FRAMEWORK EDITION

Skills in
ENGLISH

1

Lindsay McNab

Imelda Pilgrim

Marian Slee

Literacy consultant: Jacqui Buckley

Heinemann Educational Publishers
Halley Court, Jordan Hill, Oxford, OX2 8EJ
A division of Reed Educational & Professional Publishing Ltd

Heinemann is a registered trademark of Reed Educational & Professional Publishing Ltd

OXFORD   MELBOURNE   AUCKLAND
JOHANNESBURG   BLANTYRE   GABORONE
IBADAN   PORTSMOUTH NH (USA)   CHICAGO

© Sections A–E: Lindsay McNab, Imelda Pilgrim, Marian Slee 2001
© Section F: Jacqui Buckley, Imelda Pilgrim 2001

First published 2001
05   04   03   02
10   9   8   7   6   5

ISBN 0 435 19282 5

Designed by 320 Design. Produced by Gecko Ltd, Bicester, Oxon

Printed and bound in Spain by Mateu Cromo

Original illustrations © Heinemann Educational Publishers 2001

Illustrations by Kathy Baxendale: pages 37, 107, 109, 111, 113, 118, Carey Bennett: page 90, Abigail Conway: pages 31, 63, 160, 161, Tim Davies: pages 7, 48, 98, 121, 159, 174, Nick Duffy: pages 50, 79, 82, Alice Englander: pages 11, 12, 18, 53, 57, 66, 67, 71, 83, DTP Gecko: pages 92, 122, 172, 173, Rosalind Hudson: pages 15, 16, 43, Nadime Faye-James: pages 74, 75, Chris Long: pages 87, 116, Paul McCaffrey: pages 55, 56, 106, Louise Morgan: page 70, Julian Mosedale : pages 28, 29, 46, 81, 168, Joanne Moss: pages 60, 64, Andrew Quelch: pages 30, 41, 42, 51, 73, 94, 140, Martin Sanders: page 169, Nick Schon: pages 26, 27, 84, 103, 105, 128, 154, 164,180, 186, Sarah Warburton: pages 19, 20, 35, 58, 78, 119, 124, 144, 165, 171, Rosie Woods: pages 9, 43

The publishers would like to thank the following for permission to reproduce photographs on the pages noted.

Photodisc, pp.30, 102 (bottom left and right), 108, and 139; Collections/Dorothy Burrows, p.69 (top left), Format/Melanie Friend, p.69 (top right), FLPA/Derek Middleton, p.69 (bottom left), Collections/Fay Godwin, p.69 (bottom right); Peter Morris, (top right); Hulton-Getty, p.118; PYMCA, p.158 (top right); Corbis, p.158, (top left, bottom left and bottom eight) and 167

Copyright permissions sought by Jackie Newman

Original picture research by Jennifer Johnson

Tel: 01865 888058 www.heinemann.co.uk

Introduction

> ## Words
>
> Bright is the ring of words
>   When the right man rings them,
> Fair the fall of songs
>   When the singer sings them.
> Still they are carolled and said –
>   On wings they are carried –
> After the singer is dead
>   And the maker buried.
>
> ***Robert Louis Stevenson***

WORDS ARE ALL AROUND US – written down for us to read, spoken and sung for us to listen to. We have so many words in our heads – words to write down, to be read by others, and words to speak and sing, to be listened to by others.

The study of English is about the study of words and how they are placed together. It is a study that starts when we are born and first hear the rhythms of the words spoken to us. It is a study that continues throughout our lives as we gain an ever increasing range of words and an awareness of the effects they can have.

Through this book, and the CD-ROM that accompanies it, you will develop your skills in reading, writing, speaking and listening. You will read the words of other writers, and be helped to understand their meanings and appreciate their skills. You will write your own words, be guided in your choice of the best words to use and be shown how to make the most of them. You will be involved in a range of speaking and listening activities and be advised on how to make sure your words count.

We hope you enjoy the texts and the activities that we have chosen for you and that, through them, you develop your skills in English.

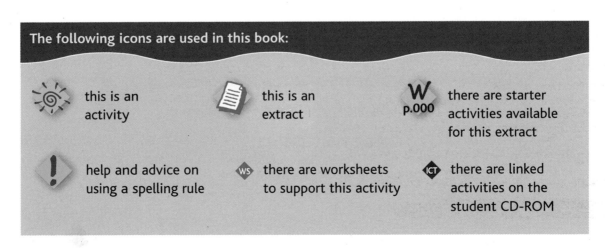

The following icons are used in this book:

this is an activity	this is an extract	**W** p.000 there are starter activities available for this extract
help and advice on using a spelling rule	WS there are worksheets to support this activity	ICT there are linked activities on the student CD-ROM

CONTENTS

Section E – Speaking and listening   154

Section F – Words: spelling strategies and vocabulary   177

ACKNOWLEDGEMENTS

The publishers gratefully acknowledge the following for permission to reproduce copyright material. Every effort has been made to trace copyright holders, but in some cases it has proved impossible. The publishers would be happy to hear from any copyright holder that has not been acknowledged.

Extract from *Le Morte D Arthur* by Thomas Malory, edited and abridged by Helen Cooper (Oxford World Classics, 1998) reprinted by permission of Oxford University Press, pp15–16; 'Little Red Riding Hood and the Wolf' from *Revolting Rhymes* by Roald Dahl, published by Jonathan Cape. Used by permission of The Random House Group Limited, pp19–20; 'It is Night' by Janice E. Parkin, originally published in T.A.S.C. Poetry, p22; 'The Washing Machine' by Jeffrey Davies, taken from *Wordspinners*, published by Oxford University Press, used with the kind permission of Mrs S. Davies, p22; 'According to my mood' from *Talking Turkeys* by Benjamin Zephaniah, published by Viking, 1994, Benjamin Zephaniah 1994. Reprinted with permission of Penguin Books Limited, p24; 'Little Blue Mini' from *Get Back Pimple* by John Agard, published by Viking in 1996. Reprinted by kind permission of John Agard c/o Caroline Sheldon Literary Agency, p24; 'Obstacles' by Lorraine Simeon reprinted by permission of the author, p25; 'At The Match. Harry's Monologue' from *Zigger Zagger* by Peter Terson © Peter Terson. Reproduced by permission of The Agency (London) Limited. All rights reserved and enquiries to The Agency (London) Limited, 24 Pottery Lane, London W11 4LZ. Fax: 0207 727 9037, p26; 'US Flies in Hamburgers' by Roger McGough, found in *A World of Poetry*, published by Kingfisher © Roger McGough. Reprinted by permission of Peters Fraser & Dunlop on behalf of Roger McGough, p28; 'The Fly' from *The Complete Poems of Walter de la Mare 1969* by Walter de la Mare. Reprinted by permission of The Literary Trustees of Walter de la Mare and The Society of Authors as their representative, p30; extract from *The Sword in the Stone* by T. H. White, published by HarperCollins Publishers Limited, used with permission of the Publisher, pp33–34; extract from *Buddy* by Nigel Hinton, © Nigel Hinton 1982. Reproduced with permission of Curtis Brown Limited, London, on behalf of Nigel Hinton, p35; Illustration by Quentin Blake from *The Witches* by Roald Dahl, published by Jonathan Cape. Used by permission of The Random House Group Limited, p39; extract from *The Witches* by Roald Dahl, published by Jonathan Cape and Penguin Books. Reprinted by permission of David Higham Associates Limited, pp39–40; extracts from *Harry Potter and the Philosopher's Stone* by J. K. Rowling, © J. K. Rowling 1997. Reprinted by permission of Christopher Little Agency, pp41–42, p73; extract from *Rice without Rain* by Minfong Ho, © Minfong Ho. Reprinted by permission of A. M. Heath & Co. Limited, p43–44; extract from *Street Child* by Berlie Doherty, published by HarperCollins Publishers, used with permission of the Publisher, pp46–47; extract from *Out of Everywhere* by Marilyn Watts, from *The Young Oxford Book of Aliens* edited by Dennis Pepper published by Oxford University Press, © Marilyn Watts, 1998. Reprinted by permission of the author, p50; extract from *Patchwork* from *Ghostly Companions* by Vivien Alcock, published by Mammoth 1994, © Vivien Alcock 1984. Reprinted by permission of John Johnson (Authors' Agent) Limited, p50; extract from *Goodman's Tenants* by Michael Chislett. Reprinted by permission of the author, p51; *Home From Sea* from *Short!* by Kevin Crossley-Holland, published by Oxford University Press 1998, © Kevin Crossley-Holland, 1998. Reprinted by permission of the author and the publishers, pp53–55; extract from *How Green You Are* by Berlie Doherty. Reprinted by permission of David Higham Associates Limited, p58; extracts from *Goodnight Mr. Tom* by Michelle Magorian, published by Penguin, © Michelle Magorian 1981. Reproduced by permission of the author c/o Rogers Coleridge & White Limited, 20 Powis Mews, London W11 1JN, pp59–60; text from *Dark, Dark Tale* by Ruth Brown. Reprinted by permission of Andersen Press Limited and the author p63; extract from *Tuck Everlasting* by Natalie Babbitt, © Natalie Babbitt 1975. Reprinted by permission of Farrar, Straus and Giroux LLC, p64; extracts from *Skellig* by David Almond, published by Hodder & Stoughton Limited, © 1998 David Almond. Reprinted by permission of Hodder & Stoughton Limited, p67; extract from *Granny Was a Buffer Girl* by Berlie Doherty, © 1986 Berlie Doherty, published by Methuen Children's Books and Mammoth, imprints of Egmont Children's Books Limited and used with permission, p70; extract from *The Woman in Black* by Susan Hill, published by Vintage, © Susan Hill 1983. Reprinted by permission of Sheil Land Associates Limited, p71; 'The Sound Collector' from *You Tell Me* by Roger McGough, published by Kestrel, © Roger McGough. Reprinted by permission of Peters Fraser & Dunlop on behalf of Roger McGough, p79; 'Alligator' by Spike Milligan. Reprinted by permission of Spike Milligan Productions Limited, p81; extract from 'Octopus or Octopuss' by Stewart Henderson, © Stewart Henderson 1994. Reprinted by the kind permission of the author, p82; extract from 'Fireworks' from *Complete Poems for Children* by James Reeves, published by Heinemann. Reprinted by permission of Laura Cecil Literary Agency on behalf of the James Reeves Estate, p82; extract from 'On Roofs of Terry Street', taken from *Terry Street* by Douglas Dunn, published by Faber and Faber Limited, p82; extract from 'Cleaning Ladies' by Kit Wright, from *Hot Dog and other Poems* by Kit Wright (Kestrel, 1981), © Kit Wright 1981. Reprinted by permission of the author and Penguin Books Limited, p82; extract from 'The Butcher' from *The Onion Memory* by Craig Raine, © Craig Raine 1978. Reprinted by permission of David Godwin Associates, p82; extract from 'Badlanders' by Christopher Reid. Reprinted with permission of the author, p82; 'A Simile Riddle' by Stanley Cook. Reprinted with permission of Sarah Matthews, p84; extract from NSPCC letter, reproduced with the kind permission of the NSPCC, p89; extract from 'Chinese Puzzle Over William The Fish' which appeared in Daily Express 12.2.98. Reprinted by permission of Wessex Features & Photos Limited, p89; Swimming-pool timetable taken from Hambledon Leisure Centre's leaflet. Reproduced with the kind permission of Hambledon District Council, p89; 'Bear's Breakfast Recipe' from *The Teddy Bear Cookbook*, © Octopus Books Limited 1986. First published by Dean, an imprint of Egmont Children's Books Limited, and used with permission, p89; extract from *Exploring Home Economics Bk 1* by Ruth Riddell, Lorraine Scott and Lynn Rogers, 2nd Edition, 1988 Addison Wesley Longman, Australia. Reproduced by permission of Pearson Education, Australia, p90; extract and photos from *Worldview 1* by Fred Martin and Aubrey Whittle, reprinted by permission of Heinemann Educational, p91; extracts from *See Through History – The Vikings* by Anne Pearson, reprinted by permission of Heinemann Educational, p93, p95; extract from Sea Life Centre leaflets reproduced with the kind permission of Merlin Entertainments Group, p97; Opening page from the Leeds United website reproduced with the kind permission of Leeds United Football Club, p100; extract from www.mykindaplace.com, reproduced with the kind permission of mykindaplace.com, p100; Guide Association Advert, reproduced with the kind permission of The Guide Association, p101; Index from *Usborne World of the Unknown* reproduced from *World of the Unknown UFOs* by permission of Usborne publishing, © 1989, 1977, Usborne Publishing Limited, p180; extracts from *Alien Abduction* by permission of Usborne Publishing © 1997 Usborne publishing Limited; extracts from *Hotshots-UFOs* by permission of Usborne Publishing © 1996, 1995, 1992, 1977 Usborne Publishing Limited, p109; extract 'The man who took on Jaws .... and survived' from *Today* Newspaper 14.6.95, © News International used with permission, p115; photo of 'The man who took on Jaws .... and survived', reproduced with the kind permission of South West News Service; extract on bicycles from *The Macmillan Encyclopedia*, published by Macmillan p117; Scaredy Cat instructions, reproduced with the kind permission of Orchard Toys, p122; Pass the Bomb instructions, reproduced by permission of H.P. Gibson and Sons Ltd, p123; Map from *Walks around Keswick*, © Footprint 1996 reprinted by kind permission of Stirling Surveys, p124; Blackpool Sea-Life Centre map, reproduced by permission of Merlin Entertainments Group, p125; CRISIS Leaflet, reproduced with the kind permission of CRISIS, p134; Atari advert © Hasbro Europe, p.136; Sea Life advert reproduced with the kind permission of Merlin Entertainments Group, p137; extract from 'Are computers bad for you?' from June 2nd 2000 issue of www.thenewspaper.org.uk, p149; 'Camelot Theme Park' brochure reproduced with the kind permission of Camelot Theme Park, pp151–152; Extract from *The Iron Woman* by Ted Hughes, published by Faber and Faber Limited, reprinted by permission of the publishers, pp160–161; extract from *War of the Worlds* by Howard Koch. Reprinted with the kind permission of Mrs Anne Koch c/o Norman G. Rudman, p167; extract from *The Art of Paper Folding* by Robert Harbin, © 1968 Robert Harbin, first published by Hodder & Stoughton Limited pp172–173.

Section A ◆ Reading literature
Introduction

The word literature has a number of different meanings. In this book it is used to describe the range of written material that is linked with the imagination and making things up.

In Year 6 you will have read a range of literature and poetry by writers past and present. You will have explored how writers craft stories and poems, and how you respond to them.

You will be developing your reading skills in the three units of work in this section.

In Unit 1, *Exploring traditional tales*, you will think about the significance and familiar features of these stories, consider how language has changed over time and examine a new version of a very old tale.

In Unit 2, *Finding ways into poetry*, you will develop your understanding and appreciation of a range of poetic forms and techniques. You will think about both the effects and the effectiveness of words when placed in a particular order.

In Unit 3, *Understanding the writer's craft*, you will explore the different ways in which writers create characters and settings. You will look at the ways these are shown to the reader and will develop your awareness of contrasts within texts.

Unit 4 tests you on the skills you will develop as you work carefully through the three units.

Reading is to the mind what exercise is to the body.
SIR RICHARD STEELE
1672–1729

This unit will help you to:

◆ develop an active reading approach
◆ explore the importance of traditional tales
◆ develop an awareness of changes in language over time
◆ think about how traditional tales can be changed.

Thinking about stories

What makes writers want to write? Do you think they want to:

◆ pass on knowledge
◆ explain an idea
◆ entertain their readers?

What other reasons can you think of?

There are millions of books and millions of writers, both past and present. Most people who write do so because they have ideas that they want to communicate to others.

But what happened before there were books? How did people express their ideas when they had no pens, no paper and no written language? The answer is that they told stories; before there were books, and for many years after, storytelling was an important way of passing on knowledge and beliefs.

Myths

There are different types of traditional stories: one of these types is **myth**. This is an English term which comes from the Greek word *mythos* meaning *word*, *saying* or *story*.

Across the world, peoples of the past told stories. Sometimes these stories were about powerful gods and goddesses who governed the lives of humans. The story on the next page comes from Ancient Greece.

Activity 1 WS ICT

Copy this note frame and prompts. When you have read the story, make notes under the headings (some have been started for you). This will help you to check your understanding of the story.

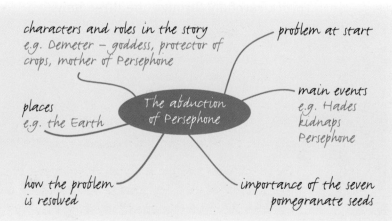

characters and roles in the story
e.g. Demeter – goddess, protector of crops, mother of Persephone

places
e.g. the Earth

The abduction of Persephone

problem at start

main events
e.g. Hades kidnaps Persephone

how the problem is resolved

importance of the seven pomegranate seeds

p.182

The Abduction of Persephone

The goddess Demeter protected the crops and soil for mankind. She had a beautiful daughter called Persephone, whom she loved more than anything in the whole world. Persephone's father was Zeus, the ruler of all the gods. Zeus had a brother called Hades who was the god of the Underworld. He had fallen in love with Persephone
5 and wanted to take her to his dark and dismal kingdom. Knowing that he would never get Zeus' permission for this, he kidnapped her one day while she was out picking flowers with some friends.

When Demeter learnt of what had happened she was desperate with grief and went to Zeus for help. Zeus explained that if Persephone had eaten so much as a mouthful
10 of food in his brother's kingdom of the dead she would be forced to remain in the Underworld for ever. He did not want to start an argument with his brother and refused to do anything. In fury, Demeter said that she would no longer protect the earth and that it would be a barren place until her daughter was returned safely.

Throughout the following year there was a terrible famine on earth. All the crops died
15 and the trees yielded no fruit. Zeus was very concerned for mankind and so sent his messenger Hermes to plead with Hades for Persephone's return. Hades pretended to agree with what Hermes said, but all the time he knew that Persephone had secretly eaten seven pomegranate seeds and that, because of this, she could not return to the world of the living.

20 When Zeus heard of this he held a conference to discuss what should be done. It was decided that Persephone's time should be shared between the two worlds; she would spend nine months of the year with her mother and the other three months with Hades in the Underworld.

And so it is that for three months every year, the cold season comes and it looks as
25 though the world has gone into mourning. Then the trees lose their leaves and nothing will grow until the spring, when Persephone is released from the darkness of the Underworld and her mother celebrates her return.

Activity 2

1 Without looking again at the story, say what agreement was finally made.

2 In the past, people would often tell stories to try to explain the mysteries of life and nature. What does this story try to explain about the natural world?

3 Try to think of, or find out about, other stories that were told to account for things that people could not understand. Collect a list of their titles and say what they try to explain.

Word bank
abduction
– kidnapping
pomegranate
– a round fruit containing many seeds

The peoples of the past did not tell stories just to explain the world around them. They also wanted to excite and entertain their listeners. When we read stories of the past, we find many of the qualities that still make a good story today.

Talk about stories you know. You may have read them or seen them on TV or as a film. Try to name some that contain one or more of the following:

- a monster or evil character
- a hero or heroine
- someone innocent being hurt by the monster
- an attempt to destroy the monster.

How do these stories usually end?

One of the earliest works in Old English is the **epic** poem *Beowulf*. An epic is a long story of heroic events and actions. *Beowulf* was first written down in the tenth century and contains many of the qualities that make a good story today. Read this extract, written in modern English.

Beowulf

p.182

There was a time when the court of King Hrothgar of Denmark rang with music and laughter. The great banqueting hall, Heorot, was the home of feasting and singing and of storytelling. All that was to change on the night our story begins …

Grendel heard the music of the harps ringing out across the fields. Curled up in the
5 darkness of the swamp, Grendel heard and one poisoned eye flickered open. Softly it growled to itself. For Grendel understood nothing of pleasure and so hated it. Hatred ruled its life. The bitterness of centuries ran in its veins, congealing its blood. In its every waking moment it writhed in a torment of self-pity and half-formed dreams of revenge. Now, hearing the sound, it slithered through the mud and began to limp
10 towards the hall.

It was at that grey time between night and day when it reached Heorot. Now, at last, the revellers were asleep, intoxicated by wine and good companionship. Grendel struck quickly and greedily. Thirty warriors were snatched up from where they lay. Thirty brave men met a brutal, cowardly death. Glutted with blood, Grendel slunk
15 away, back to the solitude of the swamp. Even in its victory, it knew no pleasure. It had done what it had set out to do: neither more nor less.

Twice more Grendel came to Heorot, each time returning in the twilight hours to claim another thirty Danish warriors. After that, the hall was closed.

A shadow had fallen across the whole country. Sometimes, in sadness, King Hrothgar,
20 who was now an old man, would return to his beloved Heorot and sit in the silence with only his memories to keep him company. It was there some twelve years later that he met Beowulf.

The king was sitting in his chair when the door of the banqueting hall crashed open. He squinted as bright
25 sunlight flooded in, capturing a million motes of dust within its golden beams. A figure stepped forward,

Word bank
congealing – thickening
motes – specks

silhouetted against the light which could almost have
been emanating from his own body. The dust formed
a shimmering aura around him. The king trembled.
30 Never had there been a warrior so tall, so strong.

Word bank
emanating – coming out
aura – halo

The stranger approached and fell onto one knee.
He was dressed in a blue cloak over a silvery mail shirt.
In one hand he carried a richly-decorated shield, in the other a spear. His helmet
masked his face but it could not hide the fair hair that tumbled down onto his shoulders
35 nor the bright blue eyes that shone despite the shadows.

'Your majesty!' the figure said. 'My name is Beowulf. I have crossed a great sea to come
before you, to serve you and to destroy the monster that brings such terror to your land.'

As we read stories we often predict what will happen next. Our predictions are based on
stories we already know and on clues given to us by the writer. Before you read on, try to
predict what will happen in this story. Use your knowledge of other stories to help you.
What clues can you find? Write down your prediction.

The king welcomed Beowulf and that night, for the first time in many years, the floors of Heorot were swept, the tables cleaned and the beacons and fires

40 relit. That night, as the Danes feasted and sang, the echoes of their voices were carried by the wind out over the swamp. Slowly they drifted until, as the fires of Heorot were dampened and sleep replaced laughter, they reached the lair of Grendel. Once again, the poisonous yellow eyes flickered open. Once again, reaching out with one hand, it pulled itself to its feet.

45 Gliding through the shadows, Grendel came. Pushing through the mists that shrouded the moors, it pressed on towards Heorot. When at last it saw the mead-hall, its pace quickened. One scaly foot came down on a twig, snapping it. Beowulf heard the sound and opened his eyes.

Grendel reached the door of Heorot.

50 At the touch of its hands, the solid wood crumpled like paper. Two flames ignited in its eyes as it stepped inside. Saliva dripped from its mouth.

Beowulf had expected it to make straight for him. But one of the young soldiers had chosen to sleep on the other side of the door, and it was this unfortunate youth that the monster seized first, tearing him into

55 pieces and swallowing them whole.

Only then, driven to a brutal frenzy by the taste of blood, did Grendel stretch out its hands and seize Beowulf.

At once it knew that it had made a fatal mistake. Even as its claws tightened, it found itself grasped with a strength that it would have

60 thought impossible in a human. Suddenly afraid, it tried to pull away, to slither back into the darkness in which it had been born, but it was too late. Its whole arm was frozen in Beowulf's grip. Struggle though it might, it could not escape.

Grendel screamed at Beowulf, their heads so close that they

65 almost touched. The monster who had never once in its life known fear had now discovered terror. It had to get away, away from the impossible man who still held it in a savage grip. And away it went – snapping the tendons in its own shoulder, unlocking the bones and tearing the skin.

70 Howling with pain, it fled from Heorot, back into the night, blood gushing from the horrible wound that it had inflicted on itself.

Word bank
ignited – caught fire
tendons – bands of tissue attaching muscles to bones

And inside the hall, Beowulf held the dreadful trophy of his victory. It was the monster's hand, its arm, its entire torn-off shoulder. These he hung beneath the gable
75 of the roof. Heorot was cleansed. Never again would the creature return.

For Grendel was dying. Even as it fled, sobbing through the night, its life-blood was flowing out of it. By the time it reached its home in the swamp, it was cold, colder than it had ever been before. Tears flowed from its eyes as it buried its raw jagged shoulder in the mud, trying to ease the pain.

80 When dawn finally came, it was dead. It had died miserably, alone in its lair, and its soul had been welcomed in Hell.

Activity 3 (ws)

1 Look back at your prediction. Were you right? What clues in the first part of the story helped you? How did your knowledge of other stories help you?

2 Re-read lines 4–10 and lines 27–37. Try to picture Grendel and Beowulf. List the words and phrases that the writer uses to make:

- ◆ Grendel seem evil
- ◆ Beowulf seem good.

Notice how these characters are either good or bad, not a mixture of both.

3 The story starts to build to its climax at line 58, with the fight between Beowulf and Grendel. The writer chooses verbs like *tightened* and *grasped* to create a sense of drama and excitement. Here he is using the *–ed* form of the verbs. Now re-read the climax of the story:

And away it went – <u>snapping</u> the tendons in its own shoulder, <u>unlocking</u> the bones and <u>tearing</u> the skin. <u>Howling</u> with pain, it fled from Heorot, back into the night, blood <u>gushing</u> from the horrible wound that it had inflicted on itself.

What form of verbs does the writer use here? Talk about why you think the writer does this.

Activity 4 (ws)

1 Copy lines 76–81. Underline the verbs in these lines. What do you notice about the changing forms of the verbs used by the writer?

2 How does this ending make you feel about Grendel? Highlight the words in lines 76–81 which help to make you feel this way.

Look at this sentence from the climax in *Beowulf*:

> *Even as its claws tightened, it found itself grasped with a strength that it would have thought impossible in a human.*

The underlined part of the sentence before the comma tells us something extra about the monster. It is separate from the main clause and forms a subordinate clause. The writer gives this extra information to help create a clearer picture of what is happening.

This subordinate clause can be moved around within the sentence:

> *It found itself, even as its claws tightened, grasped with a strength that it would have thought impossible in a human.*
>
> *It found itself grasped with a strength, even as its claws tightened, that it would have thought impossible in a human.*

Notice how the focus of a sentence can change depending on where the subordinate clause is placed.

Activity 5

1   How many different ways can you find of writing these sentences by moving the underlined subordinate clauses? Your sentences must still make clear sense.

Suddenly afraid, it tried to pull away, to slither back into the darkness in which it had been born, but it was too late.

Struggle though it might, it could not escape.

Howling with pain, it fled from Heorot, back into the night, blood gushing from the horrible wound that it had inflicted on itself.

2   Look at each of the sentences you have created. How does moving the subordinate clause change the focus or emphasis of each sentence?
    When writing your own stories you can:

    ◆ choose your verbs to create a sense of drama and excitement
    ◆ use the –ing form of the verb to make the action more immediate
    ◆ use subordinate clauses to give extra information
    ◆ vary where you place the subordinate clauses in your sentences for effect.

Legends ⬦

A **legend** is another type of traditional story. Like a myth, it is a story passed on by word of mouth. The main difference is that a legend is thought to be based on real people and real events.

One very famous legend is that of King Arthur and the Knights of the Round Table. Adapted from French stories by Sir Thomas Malory, and printed on Caxton's press in 1485, this legend continues to have an impact on modern-day writing, film-making and music.

Activity 6 ⬦

Make a spider diagram to show all the things you know about King Arthur and the Knights of the Round Table.

The words in **bold** below are often linked with Arthur. Did you have them on your spider diagram? If not, add them to it.

The legend of King Arthur is probably based on a fifth-century **warrior** called Arthur, who united the Britons against the Saxons. According to the legend, Arthur became king when he pulled a **sword from a stone**. Over the years that followed he gathered around him at **Camelot** many **brave and noble knights**, who had many great **adventures**.

This next story tells of how Arthur came by his famous sword, **Excalibur**, whilst out riding with the **magician, Merlin**. As you read, try to get a general understanding of the passage.

Le Morte D'Arthur

And as they rode, King Arthur said, 'I have no sword.'
'No force,' said Merlin, 'hereby is a sword that shall be yours, and I may.'
So they rode till they came to a lake that was a fair water and broad.
5 And in the midst Arthur was ware of an arm clothed in white samite, that held a fair sword in that hand.
'Lo,' said Merlin, 'yonder is the sword that I spoke of.'
So with that they saw a damosel going upon the lake.
'What damosel is that?' said Arthur.
10 'That is the Lady of the Lake,' said Merlin. 'And within that lake there is a great rock, and therein is as fair a palace as any on earth, and richly beseen. And this damosel will come to you anon; and then speak ye fair to her that she may give you that sword.'

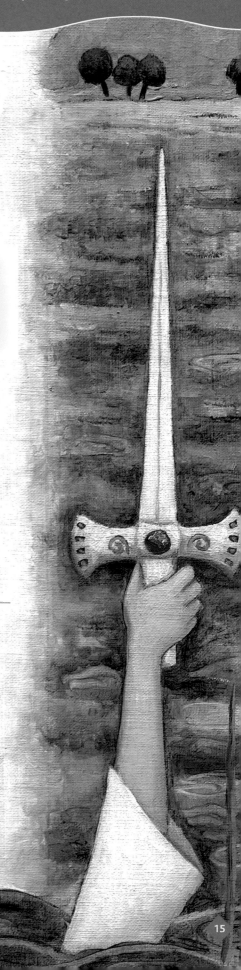

So anon came this damosel to Arthur and saluted him, and he
15 her again.

'Damosel,' said Arthur, 'what sword is that yonder that the arm holdeth above the water? I would it were mine, for I have no sword.'

'Sir Arthur,' said the damosel, 'that sword is mine. And if ye will give me a gift when I ask it you, ye shall have it.'

20 'By my faith,' said Arthur, 'I will give you what gift ye will ask.'

'Well,' said the damosel. 'Go ye into yonder barge and row yourself to the sword, and take it and the scabbard with you; and I will ask my gift when I see my time.'

So King Arthur and Merlin alit and tied their horses unto two trees,
25 and so they went into the barge; and when they came to the sword that the hand held, then King Arthur took it up by the handles and bore it with him, and the arm and the hand went under the water. And so he came unto the land and rode forth.

Then King Arthur looked on the sword and liked it passing well.
30 Then said Merlin, 'Whether like ye better the sword or the scabbard?'

'I like better the sword,' said Arthur.

'Ye are the more unwise, for the scabbard is worth ten of the sword; for while ye have the scabbard upon you, ye shall lose no blood be ye never so sore wounded. Therefore keep well the scabbard always
30 with you.'

from **Le Morte D'Arthur** *by Sir Thomas Malory*

You may not have recognised some of the words in the passage because:

◆ you have not learned them yet, for example, *samite* in line 5
  (this was a heavy silk material used for clothing in the Middle Ages)
◆ the words are archaic and rarely used now, for example, *ye*, first used
  in line 13. Today we would use *you* instead.

Activity 7 (WS) (ICT)

1   Look at lines 1–13. List the words you do not know. Try to work out their meanings by:

- ◆ looking at what comes before and after them
- ◆ thinking about words you know that are similar
- ◆ using a dictionary.

2   Try writing lines 1–13 in modern English. You do not need to do a word for word update. Try to get the general idea of what is being said, e.g. for lines 1–2 you could write:

As they were riding along, King Arthur said, 'I haven't got a sword.'
'No problem,' said Merlin, 'There's a sword near here that you can have
if I can fix it.'

3   It is not only the words in the passage that may be strange to you. You may also have noticed something unusual about:

- ◆ the way the words are used: the damosel (young woman) tells Arthur, 'Go ye into yonder barge and row yourself to the sword'. Nowadays we would probably say: 'Get in that boat and row to the sword.'
- ◆ the order in which the words are placed: when Merlin asks Arthur which he prefers, Arthur replies: 'I like better the sword.' Nowadays we would say: 'I like the sword better.'

Find and copy *three* sentences where you think words are used in an unusual way. Rewrite them as you think they might be written today.

Fairy tales

Another type of traditional story is the fairy tale.

Activity 8 (WS)

Copy and add to this diagram to help you map what you know about fairy tales. The prompts should help you think.

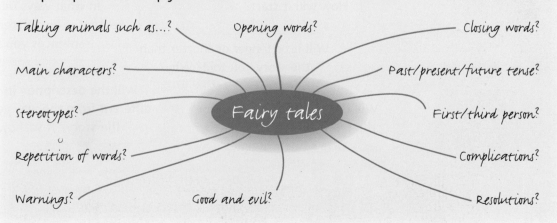

Activity 9

1 Remind yourself of the fairy tale of *Little Red Riding Hood* by listing the key points. Retell it to a friend in an interesting and lively way.

2 Here are some features found in fairy tales, which you may have discovered in Activity 8. Which of these are in the story of *Little Red Riding Hood* as you retold it?

Starts with
'Once upon a time ...'

Has a child in danger

Ends with 'And they all
lived happily ever after'

Words are
repeated several times

Has one or more of these characters:
● handsome prince ● woodcutter
● king ● evil stepmother
● fairy godmother

Involves at least one animal
that behaves like a human

The prince rescues the girl

Has a bad character who tries
to kill the good character

Good wins over evil

Something magical
happens

Something horrible happens
to the bad character

3 Before you read the fairy tale of *Little Red Riding Hood* on pages 19–20, discuss how a written version of the story might differ from the way you retold it in your spoken version.

How will it start?

In what ways might the
sentences be different from the
sentences you used?

Will it be longer or shorter than
the story you told? Why?

Will it use different words from
the ones you used? If so, why?
Give some examples.

Will the description in it be
different from the way you told
the story? If so, how?

This version of *Little Red Riding Hood* might not be written in the way you expect. It is still recognisable as the fairy tale but is different from the way it is usually told.

Activity 10 ICT

Copy and complete this chart. Read Roald Dahl's version of *Little Red Riding Hood* carefully. Think about the content and the way it is written. Complete the chart by identifying *five* ways in which his version is:

◆ similar to the traditional tale
◆ different from the traditional tale.

Similarities	Differences
1 The wolf eats the grandmother	**1** Different opening – not 'Once upon a time …'

Little Red Riding Hood and the Wolf

As soon as Wolf began to feel
That he would like a decent meal,
He went and knocked on Grandma's door.
When Grandma opened it, she saw
5 The sharp white teeth, the horrid grin,
And Wolfie said, 'May I come in?'
Poor Grandmamma was terrified,
'He's going to eat me up!' she cried.
And she was absolutely right.
10 He ate her up in one big bite.
But Grandmamma was small and tough,
And Wolfie wailed, 'That's not enough!
I haven't yet begun to feel
That I have had a decent meal!'
15 He ran around the kitchen yelping,
'I've *got* to have another helping!'
Then added with a frightful leer,
'I'm therefore going to wait right here
Till Little Miss Red Riding Hood
20 Comes home from walking in the wood.'
He quickly put on Grandma's clothes
(Of course he hadn't eaten those).
He dressed himself in coat and hat.
He put on shoes and after that
25 He even brushed and curled his hair,
Then sat himself in Grandma's chair.

In came the little girl in red.
She stopped. She stared. And then she said,

'*What great big ears you have, Grandma.*'
30 '*All the better to hear you with,*' the Wolf replied.
'*What great big eyes you have, Grandma,*'
    said Little Red Riding Hood.
'*All the better to see you with,*' the Wolf replied.

He sat there watching her and smiled.
35 He thought, I'm going to eat this child.
Compared with her old Grandmamma
She's going to taste like caviar.

Then Little Red Riding Hood said, '*But Grandma,*
    what a lovely great big furry coat you have on.'
40 'That's wrong!' cried Wolf. 'Have you forgot
To tell me what BIG TEETH I've got?
Ah well, no matter what you say,
I'm going to eat you anyway.'
The small girl smiles. One eyelid flickers.
45 She whips a pistol from her knickers.
She aims it at the creature's head
And *bang bang bang*, she shoots him dead.
A few weeks later, in the wood,
I came across Miss Riding Hood.
50 But what a change! No cloak of red,
No silly hood upon her head.
She said, 'Hello, and do please note
My lovely furry WOLFSKIN COAT.'

Little Red Riding Hood and the Wolf
from ***Revolting Rhymes*** by *Roald Dahl*

Activity 11

1 a What happens to Little Red Riding Hood in the traditional fairy tale?
    How is Roald Dahl's adaptation different?

   b How does Roald Dahl's version create a different impression of little girls?

   c How does Roald Dahl make his tale funnier than the original?

   d In what ways would you say Roald Dahl's version is more up to date than the
      traditional story?

2 Think about other fairy tales you know. Discuss ways in which they could be
    changed or adapted so that they are more up to date.

This unit will help you to:

- ◆ unlock the images in poems
- ◆ recognise a range of poetic forms
- ◆ think about how form contributes to meaning
- ◆ understand how poets use rhyme, repetition, similes and sound
- ◆ explain how a writer has achieved a particular effect.

As you work through this unit, keep a record of the poems you read and what you have learnt about them. You will need this record to complete the final activity in the unit, on page 32. Start your record by mapping what you already know about poetry. Use this model as a starting point, and add to it.

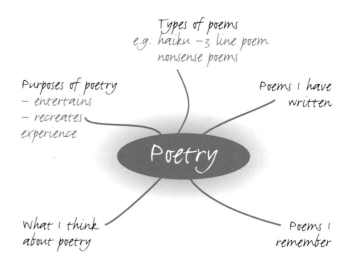

Unlocking images

Poets use words to create images in the minds of their readers. To understand a poem well, the reader needs to unlock these images.

Activity 1 ⓦⓢ

Copy this note frame. Read the poems on page 22 closely, both silently and aloud. As you read them, complete the note frame.

Poem	Picture it makes in my mind	Words that sound interesting	Interesting ideas	What it means to me
'It is Night'		'slender thread' 'a heap of light'	That the stars are just 'hanging' in the sky	

It is Night

It is night
and the stars
Hang loosely in the sky.
As if
5 at any moment
the slender thread might break
and they would fall.
Making a heap of light in
    the dark street.

Janice E. Parkin

The Washing Machine

It goes fwunkety,
    then shlunkety,
as the washing goes around.

The water spluncheses
5   and it sluncheses,
as the washing goes around.

As you pick it out it splocheses,
    then it flocheses,
as the washing goes around.

10 But at the end it schlopperies,
    and then flopperies,
and the washing stops going round.

Jeffrey Davies

Spellbound

The night is darkening round me,
The wild winds coldly blow;
But a tyrant spell has bound me
And I cannot, cannot go.

5 The giant trees are bending
Their bare boughs weighed with snow.
And the storm is fast descending,
And yet I cannot go.

Clouds beyond clouds above me,
10 Wastes beyond wastes below;
But nothing drear can move me;
I will not, cannot go.

Emily Brontë

You Say

You say I am mysterious.
Let me explain myself:
In a land of oranges
I am faithful to apples.

Elsa Gidlow

Word bank
tyrant – cruel and all powerful
drear – gloomy

Activity 2

1   In groups, talk about your ideas on the poems. Decide how you could represent each one as a picture. Make notes on a chart like this as you discuss:

   ◆   the details you would put in each picture   ◆   the colours you would use

   ◆   the reasons for your choices.

Poem	Details in picture	Reason(s)	Colours in picture	Reason(s)
'It is Night'				

2   In your reading record, list the poems and the pictures they suggested to you.

Poetic form

Poems come in all different shapes and sizes. This gives poets freedom to decide how to put their words on the page. The shape of a poem and the way the words are arranged on the page is called the **form**.

Concrete and shape poems

Sometimes poets will experiment with the way the words look on the page. They will place or write the words to give the poem visual impact. This is called **concrete poetry**.

In a **shape poem** the words are organised into the actual shape of the poem's subject.

W
p.188

Activity 3

1   Copy this chart. As you read the poems on the next page, record your thoughts.

Poem	What it's about	What's unusual about its form	Why the poet used this form
'According To My Mood'			
'Little Blue Mini'			

2   Write your own shape poem. Experiment with your choice of words and the way you place them on the page. You could choose a subject from this list:

   ◆   an aeroplane   ◆   a hand   ◆   a football   ◆   a computer   ◆   a tiger   ◆   a cup.

3   In your poetry record, explain what is meant by:
   ◆   form   ◆   concrete poetry   ◆   shape poetry.

ACCORDING TO MY MOOD

I have *poetic* **licence**, i wri**T**e th**E** way i wa**Nt**.
i *drop* my **full** stops where *i* like ...
MY CAPITAL Le**t**e**R**s go where i li**KE**,
i **order** from **MY** Pe**N**, i verse **the way** i like
5   **(i do** *my spelling write***)**
Acording to My **mo**od.
i **HA**ve **p**oetic **licence**,
i put my **commers** where **i** like,,((()).
(((my brackets are **write**((
10 **I REPEAT WH**en I lik**E**.
i can't **go** rong.
i *look* and **i.c.**
It's **rite**.
i**l REPEAT WH**en i lik**E**. i have
15 *poetic* licence!
don't question me?**?**?*?*

Benjamin Zephaniah

Word bank
poetic licence – the freedom
of poets to experiment with
the rules of language

Little Blue Mini
for Brigit

Word bank
scarab – a type of beetle
chaperone – someone who
takes care of someone else

FROM ON HIGH
it's a scarab
on the shoulder
of the motorway.
5   In a traffic jam it's a cheeky crab
inching its way towards an opening.
And when a parking place
is heaven-sent and beckoning
Who will be first to spot that welcome spa**c**e
10 **as if reserved by some lucky star?**
Who else but her little blue car
her f**o**ur wheel chaper**o**ne.

John Agard

Stanzas

Sometimes poems are organised into clearly separate blocks. These blocks are called **stanzas**. They can be short or long, the same length or different lengths.

Activity 4

Below, the lines of the poem 'Obstacles' have been mixed up. The poem has two equal stanzas of four lines. Work out the correct order of the lines in each stanza and complete this chart. The first line of each stanza is given.

Stanza 1				Stanza 2			
1	2	3	4	5	6	7	8
a				d			

Obstacles

a I can't take no more, I can't stand it
b But you are right back where you started
c When the going begins to get tough
d So you turn your back on that problem
e I tell you, I've really had enough
f How many times has this been said
g And for a while you're feeling strong
h When the next one comes along

Lorraine Simeon

Activity 5

1 Check you got the order right. The correct answers are given on page 32. If you were right, you probably used clues in the text to help you. What clues are there? It might help you to think about:

◆ what the first stanza is about ◆ what the second stanza is about
◆ the use of the first (I, we) and second (you) person ◆ the use of rhyme.

2 Now that you have thought about the poet's use of stanzas, answer this question: why do you think the poet divided the poem into two stanzas?

Free verse

Some poems are written in a less formal way. The poet may use **free verse**, which is unrhymed and does not follow a particular pattern. 'At the Match. Harry's Monologue' is an example of free verse. As you read this poem, find examples of how the poet shows Harry's excitement through the use of:

- ◆ lines of different length
- ◆ repetition
- ◆ the present tense
- ◆ the second person
- ◆ the word 'and'
- ◆ free verse.

At the Match.
Harry's Monologue

HARRY: Come Saturday,
The whole town comes alive.
People are going one way,
From all the streets,
5 They are going the one way,
And meeting and joining,
And going on and meeting more and more
Till the trickle becomes a flood.
And men are packed so tight
10 That cars have to nose their way through.
And you come to the stadium,
And it's humming,
A hum comes from the bowl.
And the people inside seem to be saying,
15 Come on in, come on in,
And you jostle at the turnstile,
And the turnstile clicks and clicks,
And push nearer and nearer,
Through the dark gap,
20 Then you're in.
And the great stand of the City End,
It's like a hall,
A great hall,
And you go on,
25 Through the arch
And you see the pitch,
Green, new shaven and watered,
And the groundsman's made
   the white lines,
As straight as a ruler,
30 And the ash is pressed.

And you find your place among the fans,
The real fans,
The singers and chanters and rattle wavers.
And a sheet of tobacco smoke hangs over the crowd.
35 And the crowd whistles and hoots,
And the policemen circling the pitch
Look up and know they're in for a rough day of it,
And the stadium fills up,
The Open End first, then the City End,
40 Then the paddock, then the covered seated stand,
Then, last of all, the fat directors
With the Lord Mayor and cigars.
And the reporters are in their little glass box,
And the cameramen position themselves
45 By the goal,
And there's a looking down the tunnel,
Then a hush.
Then out they come.
The lads,
50 Like toy footballers on a green billiard table.
And the roar goes up …

Peter Terson

Activity 6

1 Prepare a group reading of 'At the Match. Harry's Monologue'. Use your own experience of football matches or crowd scenes to help you.

In groups of three or four, study the poem carefully and decide how you could read it. Are there any lines which you could read together? Here's a model of how you might read the first eight lines aloud.

words in **bold**: more slowly or more loudly for emphasis

underlined words: more quickly

> HARRY: Come Saturday,
> The **whole** town comes alive.//
> *People are going one way,*
> From all the streets,
> *They are going the one way,*
> **And meeting and joining**,
> And going on and meeting
> more and more
> Till the trickle// becomes **a flood**.

//: pause for effect

italics: what actions could the speaker use?

underlined and in bold: all read together

Once you have thought about the choices, decide which lines each of you is going to read and how they are going to be read. Then practise your reading. You may be able to perform it for your class. If you do, notice how they respond to your reading and ask them what they thought of it. They could give you a mark out of 10, with an explanation of why they gave it to you.

2 Look back at the work you have done on stanzas and free verse. In your reading record explain:

◆ what each of these forms is

◆ why a poet might choose to use each of them.

3 Think about the different types of poetic form you have studied. Write two sentences in your reading record which explain the link between:

what the poem is about ◄───► the form the poet chooses.

Poetic devices

As well as learning about form, you need to be aware of some of the features often found in poetry. These are sometimes called **poetic devices**.

Rhyme and repetition

Roger McGough wrote the following poem after reading the newspaper headline

> **U.S. Flies in Hamburgers**

which was about hamburgers being airlifted to U.S. Marines. As you read it, think about the ways he uses rhyme, which is the repetition of similar or identical sounds.

U.S. Flies in Hamburgers

W p.183

end rhyme

internal rhyme

If you go down the High Street today
You'll be sure of a big <u>surprise</u>.
When you order your favourite burger
With a milkshake and regular <u>fries</u>.

5 For the secret is out
I tell you no lies
They've stopped using beef
In favour of FLIES

FLIES, FLIES, big juicy FLIES,
10 <u>FLIES</u> as American as apple <u>pies</u>.

Horseflies, from Texas, as big as your
thumb
Are sautéed with onions and served in
a bun.

Free-range bluebottles, carefully
rinsed
Are smothered in garlic, and
painlessly minced.

15 Black-eyed bees with stings intact
Add a zesty zing, and that's a fact.

Colorado beetles, ants from Kentucky,
Rhode Island roaches, and if you're
unlucky

Baltimore bedbugs (and even
horrider)
20 Leeches as squashy as peaches from
Florida.

FLIES, FLIES, big juicy FLIES,
FLIES as American as mom's apple pies.

It's lovely down in MacDingles today
But if you don't fancy flies
25 Better I'd say to keep well away
Stay home and eat Birds' Eyes.

Roger McGough

Word bank
sautéed – shallow-fried
roaches – cockroaches

Activity 7

Rhyme

1 Words rhyme when the same sound is repeated. Examples of **end rhyme** (lines ending in the same sound) and **internal rhyme** (rhyming words in the same line) are highlighted for you in the poem opposite. How many more examples of end rhyme and internal rhyme can you find? List them.

2 Can you think of *three* reasons why Roger McGough has used rhyme in this poem? Write them down as *Reasons for using rhyme in poetry*.

Repetition

3 Poets often repeat words, phrases (groups of words) and whole lines in poems. They may do this:

◆ to emphasise a point
◆ to create the type of chorus you might find in a song
◆ to create a sound effect, such as the motion of a train
◆ to create a particular mood, such as excitement.

Look back at 'U.S. Flies in Hamburgers'. Which lines are repeated? Why do you think the poet did this?

4 Try reading the poem aloud in small groups. Decide who will read which lines, but make sure that you all read lines 9–10 and 21–22. Notice how some words are in capital letters to make them stand out. How do you think you should read these particular words?

Think about how your class responded to your reading of 'At the Match. Harry's Monologue' (page 26). Use their responses to help you improve your reading this time.

Similes

Sometimes a poet will liken one thing to another to help create an image for the reader in order to make an idea clearer. This is known as a **simile**. In a simile you often see the words 'as' and 'like'.

Activity 8

In the poem on the next page, Walter de la Mare describes how he imagines things must look to a fly. Copy this chart and try to match the things to their similes. The first one has been done for you.

1	2	3	4	5	6	7	8
d							

The Fly

How large unto the tiny fly
Must little things appear! —

1 A rosebud like _____,
2 Its prickle like _____;
3 A dewdrop like _____,
4 A hair like _____;
5 The smallest grain of mustard-seed
   As _____;
6 A loaf of bread, _____;
7 A wasp, _____;
8 And specks of salt as bright to see
   As _____.

Walter de la Mare

a	fierce as coals of fire
b	a lofty hill
c	lambkins to a shepherd
d	a feather bed
e	a spear
f	a looking-glass
g	golden wire
h	a cruel leopard

Activity 9 (ICT)

Check your answers to Activity 8, on page 32.

1 Choose *two* of the similes you have identified. For each one, explain how it helps to create a clearer image for the reader.

2 Think about how you could use similes to describe how a giant might see things. Use the frame below, or create your own. Your lines don't have to rhyme, but they could do.

The Giant

How tiny to a towering giant
Must mighty things appear!
An ocean like _____
Its waves like _____
A cathedral like _____
A mountain like _____

The tallest trees within the forest
like _____
A jumbo jet, a _____
A lake, a _____
And skyscrapers that touch the stars
as _____

3 When you have finished, compare your simile poem with others in the group. Decide which are the best similes and why.

Word sounds

Poets use words in unusual ways and experiment with sounds. Sometimes they use words that sound like the sound they are describing, such as 'pop'. This is called **onomatopoeia**.

In this poem, the poet is trying to capture the sound and the feeling of walking in thick mud. List the words he uses to describe these sensations. Read the poem aloud for full effect.

Muddy Boots

p.184

Trudging down the country lane,
Splodgely thlodgely plooph,
Two foot deep in slimy mud.
Fallomph Polopf Gallooph.
5   Hopolosplodgely go your boots,
Slopthopy gruthalamie golumph.
Then you find firm ground again,
Plonky shlonky clonky.
BUT ... then you sink back in again,
10 Squelchy crathpally hodgle.

Sitting outside scraping your boots,
Sclapey gulapy criketty,
Cursing the horrible six inch slodge,
Scrapey flakey cakey.
15 Flakes of mud, crispling off the boots,
Crinkey splinky schlinkle.
Never again, will I venture into that
... Schlodgely, Flopchely, Thlodgely,
schrinkshely, slimy, grimy, squelchy, ghastly MUD!

Philip Paddon

Activity 10 (WS)

1 Sort the words you have listed into three groups:

◆ words you can find in the dictionary, e.g. slimy (line 3)
◆ words that are similar to ones you can find in the dictionary, e.g. Splodgely (line 2)
◆ words that are made up, e.g. gruthalamie (line 6).

2 Think about the words that describe being two foot deep in mud:

Fallomph Polopf Gallooph

and the words that describe being on firm ground again:

Plonky shlonky clonky.

   a What is the difference in the sound of the two sets of words?
   b How do the sounds of the words emphasise what is being described?

3 For each of the following choose *five* words **and** make up *five* words that describe the sounds and feelings linked with:

◆ running through water
◆ cooking a meal
◆ being in the playground at breaktime.

Activity 11 (ICT)

1 Look back at the work you have done on rhyme, repetition, simile and onomatopoeia. List these poetic devices in your poetry record. Explain what each one is and give an example of how it can be used.

2 Use the notes you have made in your reading record to help you write 'A beginner's guide to writing poetry'. This should be full of hints and examples, showing your readers the different techniques they could use.

Answers
Activity 4 (p.25): 1a, 2e, 3f, 4c, 5d, 6g, 7b, 8h; Activity 8 (p.30), 1d, 2e, 3f, 4g, 5a, 6b, 7h, 8c.

3 Understanding the writer's craft

This unit will help you to:

- ◆ **learn about different techniques used by writers**
- ◆ **understand how words can describe atmosphere**
- ◆ **refer to the text when explaining viewpoint**
- ◆ **understand how choice of words affects meaning**
- ◆ **learn about the writer's craft.**

Describing people

Writers give a lot of time and thought to the way they describe people. They want to make them seem real to the reader. To do this, they must choose their words very carefully. In this section you will examine some of the different ways writers describe people.

Sometimes writers describe the appearance of a character in great detail.

You may have already met the character of Merlin in *Le Morte D'Arthur* on pages 15–16. Read this description of the wizard Merlyn (Merlin) closely, and try to picture him clearly in your mind.

The Sword in the Stone

pp.185–186

The old gentleman was a singular spectacle. He was dressed in a flowing gown with fur tippets which had the signs of the zodiac embroidered all over it, together with various cabalistic signs, as of triangles with eyes in them, queer crosses, leaves of trees, bones and birds and animals and a planetarium whose stars shone like bits of
5 looking glass with the sun on them. He had a pointed hat like a dunce's cap, or like the headgear worn by ladies of that time, except that the ladies were accustomed to have a bit of veil floating from the top of it. He also had a wand of lignum vitae, which he had laid down in the grass beside him, and a pair of horn-rimmed spectacles. They were extraordinary spectacles, being
10 without ear pieces, but shaped rather like scissors or the antennae of the tarantula wasp.

> **Word bank**
> **singular spectacle** – unusual sight
> **tippets** – a trim on sleeves and hood
> **cabalistic signs** – secret signs
> **planetarium** – a model of the solar system
> **lignum vitae** – (Latin) the wood of life

Merlyn had a long white beard and long white moustache which hung down on either side of it, and close inspection showed that he was far from clean. It was not that he had dirty finger-nails or anything like that, but some large bird seemed to
15 have been nesting in his hair. The old gentleman was streaked with droppings over his shoulders, among the stars and triangles of his gown, and a large spider was slowly lowering itself from the tip of his hat, as he gazed and slowly blinked at the little boy in front of him.

*from **The Sword in the Stone** by T. H. White*

Activity 1 WS ICT

What picture do you have of Merlyn in your mind?
You are going to draw and label a picture of Merlyn. Start by listing the key details.
Run your finger over the words, scanning them for key details:

◆ *gown – flowing, fur tippets, embroidered with different signs*
◆ *hat – pointed …*

Complete your list before you start your drawing.
Make sure you include all the details in your work.

Activity 2

Re-read the last paragraph and answer these questions:

1 What kind of person does Merlyn seem to be?
   Give two reasons for your answer, based on evidence from the text.
2 Would you like to meet him?
   Give reasons for your answer.

A character's appearance can tell you something about the kind of person they are. You can also work out things about them from:

◆ their thoughts and feelings   ◆ their actions

◆ the things they say   ◆ their reactions to other characters.

In this extract thirteen-year-old Buddy is about to go to school with his dad to meet his teacher, Mr Normington. As you read, list the words and phrases that show:

◆ how Buddy's dad thinks and feels about his appearance

◆ how Buddy thinks and feels about his dad's appearance. Use a chart like the one below for your list.

How Buddy's dad thinks and feels about his appearance	How Buddy thinks and feels about his dad's appearance
'he'd taken great care'	'thought he was going to die'

Buddy

Buddy thought he was going to die when his dad came downstairs ready to go at six-thirty. He was dressed in his complete Teddy Boy outfit – drainpipe trousers, drape jacket with velvet collar, bootlace tie, thick crepe-soled shoes and fluorescent green socks. His hair was slicked
5 back with oil and it was obvious that he'd taken great care to look as tidy as possible. He'd dressed himself in his 'best' for the occasion.

'I thought you had to go straight out afterwards,' Buddy said, not daring to come to the point but hoping his dad might change his mind and put on something else. Jeans – anything would be better than this.

10 'I am. Got me other stuff in 'ere,' he said, holding up a Woolworth's plastic bag.

Buddy's stomach turned to water and he felt sick. The evening was going to be a disaster. 'Dad,' he said weakly.

'What?'

'Can't you put something else on?'

15 'Why?'

'Well, it's just ... Mr Normington ... won't like it.'

'He'll 'ave to lump it then, won't he?' There was defiance in his dad's voice but a touch of sadness, too, and Buddy knew he'd hurt him.

The walk to school seemed to take ages. His dad was right.
20 What did it matter what Mr Normington thought? It wasn't as if his dad looked scruffy or dirty – he looked really smart. But he did look different. Even some of the people in the street looked twice as they walked past.

*from **Buddy** by Nigel Hinton*

Activity 3

Use the lists you made while reading to help you answer these questions:

1 What do the clothes show about Buddy's dad?

2 How do you know Buddy's dad has made a special effort?

3 How do you think Buddy's dad felt when Buddy asked him to change his clothes?

4 What different things does Buddy think about his dad's appearance?

5 What are your views on what the writer, Nigel Hinton:

- ◆ thinks about the way Buddy's dad is dressed
- ◆ thinks about Buddy's reaction
- ◆ is trying to show us about the relationship between Buddy and his dad?

In the next description, Charles Dickens uses detail to focus on the kind of person Scrooge is. However, it's easy to see what he might look like from the author's imaginative use of words. The depth of detail given here is a typical feature of Dickens' writing.

As you read, try to form a picture of Scrooge's face in your mind. As soon as you finish reading, quickly draw a picture of the face you see. Explain to the person next to you why you think he looks like that.

A Christmas Carol

Oh! but he was a tight-fisted hand at the grindstone. Scrooge!
A squeezing, wrenching, grasping, scraping, clutching, covetous, old sinner! Hard and sharp as flint, from which no steel had ever struck out generous fire; secret, and self-contained, and solitary as an
5 oyster. The cold within him froze his old features, nipped his pointed nose, shrivelled his cheek, stiffened his gait; made his eyes red, his thin lips blue; and spoke out shrewdly in his grating voice. A frosty rime was on his head, and on his eyebrows, and his wiry chin. He carried his own low temperature always about with him; he iced his
10 office in the dog-days, and didn't thaw it one degree at Christmas.

External heat and cold had little influence on Scrooge. No warmth could warm, no wintry weather chill him. No wind that blew was bitterer than he, no falling snow was more intent upon its purpose, no pelting rain less open to entreaty. Foul weather didn't know
15 where to have him. The heaviest rain, and snow, and hail, and sleet, could boast of the advantage over him in only one respect. They often 'came down' handsomely and Scrooge never did.

*from **A Christmas Carol** by Charles Dickens*

Word bank

covetous – envious of other people's possessions
gait – way of walking
frosty rime – white hair
dog-days – hot summer days
'came down' handsomely –
a) fell heavily
b) gave money generously

Activity 4 WS

In this activity you will examine the techniques Dickens uses to create the character of Scrooge.

1 Dickens uses **adjectives** to tell you more about Scrooge, for example:

> *Oh! but he was a <u>tight-fisted</u> hand at the grindstone. Scrooge! A <u>squeezing</u>, <u>wrenching</u>, <u>grasping</u>, <u>scraping</u>, <u>clutching</u>, <u>covetous</u>, <u>old</u> sinner!*

   a What do these adjectives tell you about Scrooge?
   b Why do you think Dickens lists the adjectives in this way?

2 In lines 11–14 Dickens uses a list and **repetition** to emphasise a point about Scrooge's character:
   a What word does the author repeat in these sentences?
   b What idea is he trying to get across to the reader?

3 Dickens uses similes to give the reader a clearer impression of Scrooge. Copy and develop these diagrams to show what these similes tell you about Scrooge:

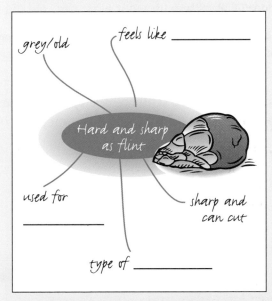

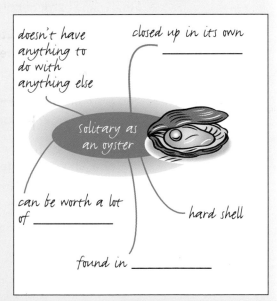

4 Dickens uses **images of coldness** to emphasise what kind of person Scrooge is.
   a List the words and phrases in the passage that link to coldness.
   b What do these add to your impression of Scrooge?

5 What is it about Scrooge that Dickens appears to dislike? What does this tell you about the things Dickens thinks are important?

6 Dickens created the character of Scrooge in *A Christmas Carol* in 1843. Can you think of any reasons why people today are still fascinated by the character of Scrooge?

Charles Dickens wrote in the nineteenth century, when writers often used long, detailed sentences to get their ideas across to their readers.

Activity 5

Read this sentence:

> *The cold within him froze his old features and spoke out shrewdly in his grating voice.*

Dickens could have left it at that. However, he chose to give his reader much more detail about the effects of the cold on Scrooge. Re-read this sentence:

> *The cold within him froze his old features, <u>nipped his nose, shrivelled his cheek, stiffened his gait; made his eyes red, his thin lips blue;</u> and spoke out shrewdly in his grating voice.*

1 How many extra details does Dickens give us about what the cold did to Scrooge?

2 A semicolon (;) is a form of punctuation used to show a pause half-way between a comma and a full stop. Dickens uses two semicolons in this sentence. Find them. Why do you think he chose to use them here?

3 You are going to write your own extended sentence. Using Dickens' description of Scrooge as a model, you are going to build a picture of warmth, not cold. Follow these stages:

  ◆ Think about the effect of warmth and sunshine on these features:
    Nose
    Cheek
    Gait (way of walking)
    Eyes
    Lips
    Voice.
  ◆ Make a note of your ideas
  ◆ Draft your sentence, starting with these words:

> *The sunshine within him warmed his old features, …*

  ◆ Read your sentence carefully. Can you improve it by changing or adding words? Have you remembered to use commas and semicolons?

Sometimes writers will use **contrast** to emphasise something about the appearance of a character. This means that they will show a character in two very different ways. In this passage a young boy, Luke, is hiding in a hall filled with witches.

Activity 6

Copy this chart and list the details in lines 1–8 which help you to form an impression of the woman. Keep the second column free for Activity 7.

Details in lines 1–8	Details in lines 21–24
She was tiny	

The Witches

W
p.187

All the women, or rather the witches, were now sitting motionless in their chairs and staring as though hypnotised at somebody who had suddenly appeared on the platform. That somebody was another woman.

The first thing I noticed about this woman was her size. She was tiny, probably no
5 more than four and a half feet tall. She looked quite young, I guessed about twenty-five or six, and she was very pretty. She had on a rather stylish long black dress that reached right to the ground and she wore black gloves that came up to her elbows. Unlike the others, she wasn't wearing a hat.

She didn't look to me like a witch at all, but she couldn't possibly *not* be one,
10 otherwise what on earth was she doing up there on the platform? And why, for heaven's sake, were all the other witches gazing at her with such a mixture of adoration, awe and fear?

Very slowly, the young lady on the platform raised her hands to her face. I saw her gloved fingers unhooking something behind her ears, and then … then she
15 caught hold of her cheeks and lifted her face clean away! The whole of that pretty face came away in her hands!

It was a mask!

What clues are given to make you think there is something suspicious about the woman? What are the effects of the ellipsis and exclamation marks in lines 14–17?

Now turn to the next page and read on:

As she took off the mask, she turned sideways and placed it carefully upon a small table near by, and when she turned round again and faced us, I very nearly screamed
20 out loud.

That face of hers was the most frightful and frightening thing I have ever seen. Just looking at it gave me the shakes all over. It was so crumpled and wizened, so shrunken and shrivelled, it looked as though it had been pickled in vinegar. It was a fearsome and ghastly sight. There was something terribly wrong with it, something
25 foul and putrid and decayed. It seemed quite literally to be rotting away at the edges, and in the middle of the face, around the mouth and cheeks, I could see the skin all cankered and worm-eaten, as though maggots were working away in there.

There are times when something is so frightful you become mesmerised by it and can't look away. I was like that now. I was transfixed. I was numbed. I was
30 magnetised by the sheer horror of this woman's features. But there was more to it than that. There was a look of serpents in those eyes of hers as they flashed around the audience.

I knew immediately, of course, that this was none other than The Grand High Witch herself. I knew also why she had worn a mask. She could never have moved around
35 in public, let alone book in at an hotel, with her real face. Everyone who saw her would have run away screaming.

*from **The Witches** by Roald Dahl*

Activity 7 ⓦ

In this activity you will explore how the author uses contrast to emphasise the horror of The Grand High Witch's real face.

1 a Re-read lines 21–25. On your chart list the details which, for you, best describe her now that she has taken the mask off.

   b Complete these sentences to show the contrast in the ways she is described:
      ◆ In line 5 she is described as looking 'quite young' but in lines 22–23 her face is described as being _____ .
      ◆ In line 6 we are told 'she was very pretty' but now _____ .

2 One of the reasons many children and adults love to read Roald Dahl is because of his descriptions of the absurd and the grotesque. Re-read lines 23–27. What words does the author use to get across a grotesque image of decay?

3 In the first part Luke says, 'She didn't look like a witch at all.' Look at his reaction to her in lines 29–30. How does the author emphasise the contrast in Luke's reaction?

In examining how writers describe people you have considered:

◆ the use of detail in describing appearance
◆ the way appearance, speech, actions and reactions can suggest character
◆ the way detail on character can give clues about appearance
◆ the use of adjectives, imagery, repetition and contrast to give more impact to a description
◆ how sentence structure can be used to emphasise points.

ICT Use what you have learned about describing people in your own writing.

Describing places

As well as taking great care to describe their characters, writers think carefully about how to describe the **setting**. The setting is the surroundings and the time in which the action takes place.

In this extract, which tells you about Harry Potter's new school, Hogwarts, Harry finds that things are not quite as he expected them to be. As you read, list the words and phrases the writer uses to create a sense of mystery and magic. The first one is underlined for you.

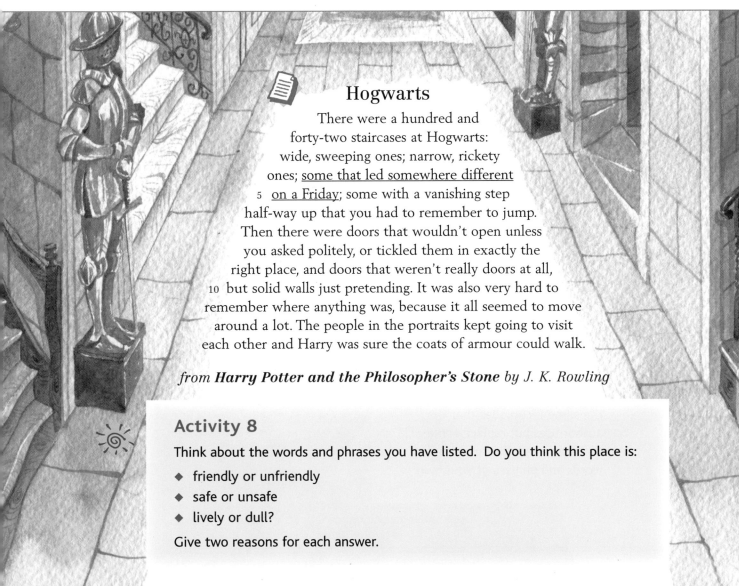

Hogwarts

There were a hundred and
forty-two staircases at Hogwarts:
wide, sweeping ones; narrow, rickety
ones; <u>some that led somewhere different</u>
5 <u>on a Friday</u>; some with a vanishing step
half-way up that you had to remember to jump.
Then there were doors that wouldn't open unless
you asked politely, or tickled them in exactly the
right place, and doors that weren't really doors at all,
10 but solid walls just pretending. It was also very hard to
remember where anything was, because it all seemed to move
around a lot. The people in the portraits kept going to visit
each other and Harry was sure the coats of armour could walk.

*from **Harry Potter and the Philosopher's Stone** by J. K. Rowling*

Activity 8

Think about the words and phrases you have listed. Do you think this place is:

◆ friendly or unfriendly
◆ safe or unsafe
◆ lively or dull?

Give two reasons for each answer.

In this next extract Harry visits the dining hall. The writer uses many of the techniques that you have seen used to describe character to describe the setting. Study the text closely and discuss the annotations that surround it.

The Dining Hall

How do Harry's thoughts help us to imagine the setting?

Find examples of adjectives used to describe the surroundings.

What kind of atmosphere does this simile help to create? How does it do this?

Harry had never even imagined such a strange and splendid place. It was lit by thousands and thousands of candles which were floating in mid-air over four long tables, where the rest of the students were sitting. These tables were
5 laid with glittering golden plates and goblets. At the top of the Hall was another long table where the teachers were sitting. Professor McGonagall led the first-years up here, so that they came to a halt in a line facing the other students, with
10 the teachers behind them. The hundreds of faces staring at them looked like pale lanterns in the flickering candlelight. Dotted here and there among the students,
15 the ghosts shone misty silver. Mainly to avoid all the staring eyes, Harry looked upwards and saw a velvety black ceiling dotted with stars.

How do people's actions let you know what kind of place it is?

What contrast does Harry's movement show us?

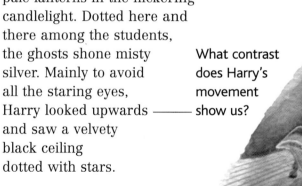

*from **Harry Potter and the Philosopher's Stone** by J. K. Rowling*

Activity 9 WS ICT

Rewrite the passage above, giving the place a frightening and dangerous atmosphere. Keep the same techniques that the author uses but replace some of the words and phrases with words and phrases of your own.

Writers sometimes show the weather to be an important feature of the setting. The novel *Rice without Rain* starts with a description of a very hot place where there has been no rain for a long time. As you read, list words and phrases that help to suggest this.

Rice without Rain

W
p.188

Heat the colour of fire, sky as heavy as mud, and under both the soil – hard, dry, unyielding.
It was a silent harvest. Across the valley, yellow rice fields stretched, stooped and dry. The sun glazed the afternoon with a heat so fierce that the distant mountains shimmered in it. The dust in the sky, the cracked earth, the shrivelled leaves fluttering on brittle
5 branches – everything was scorched.
A single lark flew by, casting a swift shadow on the stubbled fields. From under the brim of her hat, Jinda saw it wing its way west.
A good sign, Jinda thought. Maybe the harvest won't be so poor after all. She straightened up, feeling prickles of pain shoot up her spine, and gazed at the brown fields
10 before her. In all her seventeen years, Jinda had never seen a crop as bad as this one. The heads of grain were so light the rice stalks were hardly bent under their weight. Jinda peeled the husk of one grain open: the rice grain inside was no thicker than a fingernail.

*from **Rice without Rain** by Minfong Ho*

Activity 10 ⓦ

You are going to comment on the effectiveness of the description.
First, re-read the opening words: *Heat the colour of fire*
The writer creates a sense of how hot it was by saying it was 'the colour of fire'.
Imagine a fire and you start to see and feel the heat she is describing.

Now copy and complete these sentences:

In *Rice without Rain*, the sky is described as being 'as heavy as mud'. This makes me imagine the sky to be like _____ because _____.
The writer's choice of the adjectives hard, dry and unyielding, tell me that the soil is
_____.

In line 2 the harvest is described as 'silent' which could mean that _____
The word 'glazed' in line 3 means _____ . It is used by the writer to show
_____.

A sense of dryness is added to in lines 4–5 by the use of the words _____.
When describing the rice grain in line 16, the image created is _____. This image shows the reader that _____.
In conclusion, on a scale of 1–5 (1 is poor and 5 is excellent), I would give this description _____ because _____.

Towards the end of the novel the rain finally comes. There is a clear contrast between the weather here and at the start of the story. The writer uses this technique of describing the weather to emphasise the difference.

Rice without Rain

Jinda slithered down the steps of the verandah and ran towards the swinging bamboo gate. The earth was soft and pliant under her bare feet. How good to feel mud again, Jinda thought.

5   Out in the lane the wind was stronger, and a gust slashed against her arms like long sharp rice stalks. She passed the hibiscus hedge, and saw its leaves streaked a bright green where the rain had washed off the thick layers of dust. A few flowers burst through, cleansed a brilliant scarlet by the rain.

Sprinting down the lane, Jinda's steps were light and springy against the mud-slick soil. She felt the wind against her face, whipping her hair behind her, piercing
10 through her thin wet clothes so that they felt like a second skin on her ...

And still the rain quickened, pelting at the flat earth from the cloud-flattened sky.

Through the storm Jinda ran on. Running, she gulped in great mouthfuls of the wind, and felt the rain soak her clothes to her skin. Running, she felt the hard dry knot within her uncoil and grow soft and pliant again. She ran until her sides hurt,
15 and her breath came in painful gasps.

The village lay far behind. Before her the rice fields stretched out, reaching to the foot of the mountains. Bathed in wet shadow, the mountains glowed a vibrant lilac.

*from **Rice without Rain** by Minfong Ho*

Activity 11 WS ICT

1   You are going to pick out the contrasts between the two extracts. Copy and complete this table. The left-hand column contains phrases from the first extract. Find contrasts to these in the second extract and list them in the right-hand column. You will need to read carefully. The first one is done for you.

Extract 1	Extract 2
the soil – hard, dry, unyielding	The earth was soft and pliant
Across the valley, yellow rice fields stretched, stooped and dry.	
the distant mountains shimmered	
the shrivelled leaves fluttering on brittle branches	
She straightened up, feeling prickles of pain shoot up her spine	

2   In your own words, explain what changes have taken place between the extracts.

Spend about 1 hour on this.

Read each part of the extract carefully. Answer *all* the questions.

The Shilling Pie

Jim Jarvis hopped about on the edge of the road, his feet blue with cold. Passing carriages flung muddy snow up into his face and his eyes, and the swaying horses slithered and skidded as they were whipped on by their drivers. At last Jim saw his chance and made a dash for it through the traffic. The little shops in the dark street
5   all glowed yellow with their hanging lamps, and Jim dodged from one light to the next until he came to the shop he was looking for. It was the meat pudding shop. Hungry boys and skinny dogs hovered round the doorway, watching for scraps. Jim pushed past them, <u>his coin as hot as a piece of coal in his fist</u>. He could hear his stomach gurgling as the rich smell of hot gravy met him.

1   How do we know that this story is set in winter?   **3 marks**

2   What other details are you given about the setting in this paragraph?
Write about:

 ◆ the time of day
 ◆ the place
 ◆ the people
 ◆ the evidence that it was set long ago.   **8 marks**

Now read on:

10   Mrs Hodder was trying to sweep the soggy floor and sprinkle new straw down when Jim ran in.
      'You can run right out again,' she shouted to him. 'If I'm not sick of little boys today!'
      'But I've come to buy a pudding!' Jim told her. He danced up and down, opening and closing his fist so <u>his coin winked at her like an eye</u>.
15   She prised it out of his hand and bit it. 'Where did you find this, little shrimp?' she asked him. 'And stop your dancing! <u>You're making me rock like a ship at sea</u>!'
      Jim hopped onto a dry patch of straw. 'Ma's purse. And she said there won't be no more, because that's the last shilling we got, and I know that's true because I emptied it for her. So make it a good one, Mrs Hodder. Make it big, and lots of gravy!'
20   He ran home with the pie clutched to his chest, warming him through its cloth wrapping. Some of the boys outside the shop tried to chase him, but he soon lost them in the dark alleys, his heart thudding in case they caught him and stole the pie.

3 We find out about characters from what the narrator tells us and what the characters say and do. What have you found out so far about:

◆ Jim   **4 marks**

◆ Mrs Hodder?   **3 marks**

4 The three similes in the passage have been underlined. Copy them and, for each one, explain the idea the writer is trying to get across. For example:

In 'his coin as hot as a piece of coal in his fist', the idea the writer is trying to get across is _____ .   **6 marks**

(WS) **In the next question you are going to write about Jim's sisters Emily and Lizzie. Copy this chart and make notes as you read. Your completed chart will earn you up to 10 marks.**

Emily		Lizzie	
What she says/does	**What this shows about her**	**What she says/does**	**What this shows about her**
She tells Jim to be quiet	This shows she is considerate		

                                                                  10 marks

Now read the next part of the extract:

At last he came to his home, in a house so full of families that he sometimes wondered how the floors and walls didn't come tumbling down with the weight and
25 the noise of them all. He ran up the stairs and burst into the room his own family lived in. He was panting with triumph and excitement.

'I've got the pie! I've got the pie!' he sang out.

'Sssh!' His sister Emily was kneeling on the floor, and she turned round to him sharply. 'Ma's asleep, Jim.'

30 Lizzie jumped up and ran to him, pulling him over towards the fire so they could spread out the pudding cloth on the hearth. They broke off chunks of pastry and dipped them into the brimming gravy.

'What about Ma?' asked Lizzie.

'She won't want it,' Emily said. 'She never eats.'

35 Lizzie pulled Jim's hand back as he was reaching out for another chunk. 'But the gravy might do her good,' she suggested. 'Just a little taste.
Stop shovelling it down so fast, Jim. Let Ma have a bit.'

She turned round to her mother's pile of bedding and pulled back the ragged cover.

40 'Ma,' she whispered. 'Try a bit. It's lovely!'

She held a piece of gravy-soaked piecrust to her lips, but her mother shook her head and turned over, huddling her rug round her.

'I'll have it!' said Jim, but Lizzie put it on the corner of her mother's bed-rags.

'She might feel like it later,' she said. 'The smell might tempt her.'

45 'I told you,' said Emily. 'She don't want food no more. That's what she said.'

Jim paused for a moment in his eating, his hand resting over his portion of pie in case his sisters snatched it away from him. 'What's the matter with Ma?' he asked.

'Nothing's the matter,' said Emily. She chucked a log on the fire, watching how the flames curled themselves round it.

50 'She's tired, is all,' Lizzie prompted her. 'She just wants to sleep, don't she?'

'But she's been asleep all day,' Jim said. 'And yesterday. And the day before.'

'Just eat your pie,' said Emily. 'You heard what she said. There's no more shillings in that purse, so don't expect no more pies after this one.'

'She'll get better soon,' Lizzie said. 'And then she'll be able to go back to work. There's 55 lots of jobs for cooks. We'll soon be out of this place. That's what she told me, Jim.'

'Will we go back to our cottage?' Jim asked.

Lizzie shook her head. 'You know we can't go there, Jim. We had to move out when Father died.'

'Eat your pie,' said Emily. 'She wants us to enjoy it.'

60 But the pie had grown cold before the children had finished it. They pulled their rag-pile close to the hearth and curled up together, Jim between Emily and Lizzie. In all the rooms of the house they could hear people muttering and yawning and scratching. Outside in the street dogs were howling, and carriage wheels trundled on the slushy roads.

Jim lay awake. He could hear how his mother's breath rattled in her throat, and he 65 knew by the way she tossed and turned that she wasn't asleep. He could tell by the way his sisters lay taut and still each side of him that they were awake too, listening through the night to its noises, longing for day to come.

*from **Street Child** by Berlie Doherty*

5 Use your chart to help you write about the ways in which Emily and Lizzie are:

- ◆ similar   **3 marks**
- ◆ different.   **3 marks**

6 *'She'll get better soon,' Lizzie said.* (line 54)
Do you think Lizzie is right? Give clear reasons for your answer based on:

- ◆ what you know about other stories   **2 marks**
- ◆ what you know about the mother from the story   **4 marks**
- ◆ the atmosphere created by the writer in lines 60–67.   **4 marks**

       TOTAL 50 marks

Section B ◆ Writing to imagine, explore and entertain
Introduction

In this section you will be focusing on writing which is often called creative. It is the kind of writing which is associated with the imagination and making things up: stories, plays and poems. The main purposes of these kinds of writing are to entertain and explore ideas.

In Year 6 you will have compared different features and styles of writing, and written your own stories, scripts and poems.

You will be developing your writing skills in the three units of work in this section.

In Unit 5, *Writing stories*, you will learn to structure plots effectively, develop good story openings, vary sentence structures, create interesting characters and write dialogue.

In Unit 6, *Creating people and places*, you will learn about how to structure writing to involve the reader. This includes how to withhold important details, sequence sentences in paragraphs and use vocabulary imaginatively.

In Unit 7, *Playing with words*, you will use different forms of writing and experiment with language to create different effects. You will use rhyme and rhythm as well as imagery.

Unit 8 tests you on the skills you will develop as you work carefully through the three units.

5 Writing stories

This unit will help you to:

◆ **plan and structure stories**
◆ **experiment with different ways of writing**
◆ **create interesting characters**
◆ **use dialogue in prose and dramascript**
◆ **use an interesting range of sentences.**

We can watch stories in films and on television, listen to them on audio tape or the radio, read them in books and other texts. We probably all tell several stories each day – to friends and family.

Shaping stories

Openings are especially important in stories. They need to be interesting enough to 'hook' readers so that they want to continue to watch, listen or read. Different openings have different features.

Story openings

Activity 1 ⓦ

Working with a partner, match the story openings in the chart below to the appropriate features.

Feature	Story openings
1 Questions raised in reader's mind.	a In Stoneygate there was a wilderness. It was a space between the houses and the river, where the ancient pit had been.
2 A place described in a detailed, unusual or atmospheric way.	b This is the story of what happened when we sailed away from Whitegates that Friday night.
3 An unexpected event.	c I found him in the garage on a Sunday afternoon.
4 A lot of detail that makes one item seem very important.	d It was on the corner of the street that he noticed the first sign of something peculiar – a cat reading a map.
5 Clues about something that is going to happen later.	e It was a little model of an imp or a devil or something – anyway, it was a little figure of a man with horns, with one of its bronze arms down by its side and the other raised as if pointing at something.

Activity 2

1 Read these two story openings. Discuss in pairs which features listed in the chart you can find. Which opening most makes you want to read on?

2 Share with each other any instances of these features and techniques that you have used in your own stories or read in other stories.

Moving House

The house hated her. She knew that. Soon
she realized that she had always known
it, even before she moved in. But what
the house wanted wasn't the sort of
5 thing she was looking out for when she
was choosing where to live. Why should
it have been? She had asked about the bus
routes, the shops, the village hall. They all
seemed all right. She had checked the
10 neighbours. They seemed normal, decent,
friendly. She hadn't thought of checking
the house.

*from **Moving House** by Marian Abbey*

Patchwork

The tall red-brick house cast a long shadow over the lane. There was grass growing
in its gravel drive, and dandelions among the neglected roses. Behind one of the
dusty windows, an old lady could be seen dimly. Sometimes she would be gazing out
as if expecting someone to come. Sometimes her head would be bent over her
5 sewing, as if she had given up hope. Her name was Mrs Drummond, and she had
three horrible daughters.

    Horrible. It was the only word for them. They had been greedy children, Aunt
Sarah told me, cold-hearted and arrogant, taking all they could get, and demanding
more. Now their mother was old and poor, her husband dead, money and servants
10 all gone, they never came near her.

    Grey as a ghost, the old lady sat by her window all day, sewing her patchwork
quilts. Meanwhile the house crumbled about her. Tiles blew off the roof, plaster fell
from the ceilings; and still the old lady waited in vain.

*from **Patchwork** by Vivien Alcock*

Exploring a story opening in more detail

Read this opening to a supernatural story. Think particularly about how the scene is being set, and how the writer creates atmosphere and prepares the reader for what is to follow.

Goodman's Tenants

It was the first time that Dalton had visited Suffolk; the first time with his metal detector, at any rate. He walked along the shoreline, the wind from the sea blowing through his thinning, sandy hair. The wrack from yesterday's storm littered the beach, while the grey waves of the receding tide fell with a steady, sullen hiss on the sand.

5   He had long meant to try the Suffolk coast – others who shared his enthusiasm had spoken of the decent finds one might make along that ancient, haunted shore, especially in the wake of storms. The devastating tempest that had ravaged the eastern counties over the last few days had persuaded him, and he had
10 decided on impulse to drive up from London and try his luck.

    So far, two hours of walking along the shore had netted him several rusty nails, two tenpence pieces and a half-crown dated 1957. Plenty of wood lay cast about, for the storm had stirred and broken-up many old wrecks, but there was nothing that
15 could be easily identified. It was just old, rotting driftwood, black and dripping with seaweed, which lay dark and sinister on the light sand, like the hair of a drowned witch.

*from **Goodman's Tenants** by Michael Chislett*

Word bank
wrack – wreckage
washed up on the shore

Activity 3

1 Explore the details about the place given in the opening paragraphs of *Goodman's Tenants*. Make a chart with two columns to record your findings.

   a Label column 1 *Factual detail*. List the factual information which the writer includes in his description.

   b Label column 2 *Atmosphere*. Writers create different kinds of atmosphere for different purposes. They choose words and details for the effect they will have on the reader. List the words and phrases that give this place an unusual atmosphere.

2 Work with a partner to examine how the writer of *Goodman's Tenants* creates atmosphere. Put yourselves in the position of the writer. Copy and complete these sentences.

   a I used the words 'with a steady, sullen hiss' (an adverbial phrase) to describe how the waves fell. I did this to improve my description. I think they do this by _____ .

   b I made the atmosphere of the second paragraph unusual and frightening by _____ .

   c In the final sentence of the third paragraph I used several adjectives to describe the driftwood. I think the most effective adjective is _____ because _____ .

   d The final simile, in which the seaweed covering the driftwood is described as being 'like the hair of a drowned witch', works well because _____ .

3 The long final sentence in *Goodman's Tenants* can be used as a model in your own writing. Read this complex sentence, which follows its style.

It was just an old, metal piece of pipe, dull and dark with oil, which lay twisted on the concrete floor, like a waiting snake.

Write a sentence of your own following this model, describing something found in a park.

Complex sentences, which contain a lot of detail, like the one in Activity 3.3, can be used to bring variety to your writing.

Activity 4 ◉

Write your own short opening to a supernatural story. It should 'hook' the reader so that they want to read on. Think back over the techniques and ideas you have explored and choose which you will use in your own writing. Make use of the kind of sentence you created in Activity 3.3. It might go at the end of the opening paragraph, or it could be placed elsewhere.

You have been thinking about story openings. Now look at how a story can develop from an opening and reach a conclusion.

Developing a story

The following short story, *Home from the Sea*, is an example of a well shaped plot. It is broken down into sections so you can explore its different parts. Read the opening:

Home from the Sea

On Saturday morning, Jack went down to the creek. To do a bit of crabbing. To nose around in the flotsam and jetsam, and see what the tide had thrown up.

'You keep away from the edge!' said his mum.
5 'Right away! As if I hadn't got enough to worry about. No money! No food!'

Word bank
flotsam and jetsam – odds and ends washed up on the shore

Activity 5

1 This story is set by the sea. The writer does not tell you this *directly*, but which words in the first three sentences allow you to work it out?

2 What do you find out, very quickly, about the lives of Jack and his mum?

3 Think about how the story may develop. What clues are there?
Write down any clues you can find and explain what they might lead to.

Now read on:

When he rounded the corner of the Maltings, Jack saw a man sitting at one end of the jetty. That's where the little fishing-boats tied up and unloaded their lobsters and flip-flapping shiners. Well, where they used to tie up! Jack's father had been the last fisherman in those parts, but now he was drowned and food for the fishes.

'Morning!' said Jack.

But the man did not reply. He didn't even look up.

'Morning!' Jack said again. Then the man did look up. He had strings of seaweed and pieces of scruff and straw tangled up in his beard and hair. And he was wearing thigh boots and an old jersey the sea had starched and decorated with wavy patterns. Jack looked at the man's face and hands. They were white and bloated – like overcooked potatoes. In fact, they looked as if they'd burst if you poked them.

Activity 6

1   The plot has moved on. Jack has moved to the jetty and he meets another character. What new piece of information are you given about Jack?

2   A new character is introduced. In what ways does the writer make this character very different from Jack and his mum?

3   With your partner, reconsider your answer to Activity 5.3. Are there new clues which have moved your thinking on? If so, what are they?

Now continue reading the story:

25   Jack gripped his crabbing-stick and pail, and took half-a-step backwards. Then he took another. And then he turned and walked away as quickly as he dared. But when he went back round the corner of the Maltings, the sea-man was already waiting for him there. Jack could scarcely breathe. 'Excuse me!' he said loudly, much more loudly than he meant to. And then he did run.

30   Jack ran up the slip road and right back home. But at his own gate the sea-man was waiting for him. And he nodded – a sort-of-no-nonsense, come-here, do-this, follow-me nod that Jack suddenly remembered and recognised.

Activity 7

1   Until now the plot has been fairly straightforward: Jack has left his mum and gone down to the jetty. On the jetty he has encountered a strange character and spoken to him. How does this new section make the plot more complicated than it might, at first, have seemed? What happens that is strange?

2   Now explain the effect of some of the writer's choices of words and phrases and complete the following chart:

The writer's choice of words	What the reader begins to think
'Jack gripped his crabbing-stick and pail'	Jack is …
'Jack could scarcely breathe'	Jack feels …
'Jack suddenly remembered and recognised'	The 'stranger' is …

3   The writer says, 'But when he went back round the corner of the Maltings, the sea-man was already waiting for him there' instead of 'He went back round the corner of the Maltings. The sea-man was already waiting for him there.'
    Why do you think the writer began the sentence with 'But'?

Now finish the story:

35 Then the man strode straight to the garden shed. He pointed to the darkest corner, and Jack began to turn over the flower pots, rusty tins, coils of rope, and string.
Then Jack saw three gold coins, three shiners in the gloom.
'Dad!' cried Jack. 'Oh, Dad!' And he reached out …
First his father smiled that smile-round-the-corner of his. Then he began to fade, fade … He faded and Jack's
40 eyes stung with hot tears.

Home from the Sea
by Kevin Crossley-Holland

Activity 8

1 By the end of the story, various issues of the plot are resolved or sorted out. In this story there were two main issues to be resolved: the poverty and hunger of Jack and his mum, and the identity of the mysterious character on the jetty. Do you feel the resolution of this story is a good one? Explain why.

2 Think back to your work in Activity 5.3. How might this story have moved from its beginning to a *different* plot and resolution? Share your ideas with others in the class.

Working on plots

The plot of *Home from the Sea* can be broken down into the following stages:

The stages of the story	*Home from the Sea*
Stage 1 – opening: the scene is set and the main characters are introduced. There is a problem.	It is by the sea. Jack and his mum are introduced. They are very poor.
Stage 2 – developing plot: a new character is introduced, though questions are left unanswered as to who he is.	Jack sees the sea-man. He looks strange and does not respond to Jack's greeting.
Stage 3 – complication: something happens between the new character and the main character.	Jack tries to get away from the sea-man but, mysteriously, wherever Jack goes the sea-man is there.
Stage 4 – crisis: the new character forces a turning point in the story.	The sea-man lies in wait for Jack. He makes Jack follow him.
Stage 5 – resolution: we discover the identity of the mysterious character and the 'problem' at the beginning is resolved.	The sea-man reveals some hidden money to Jack, and we realise that the sea-man is the ghost of Jack's father.

Activity 9 WS ICT

1 Working with a partner, discuss how you could use the five stages to develop a *different* plot from that of *Home from the Sea* – nothing to do with Jack and his father and the sea. Your story might still be a ghost story or it could be quite different. Jot down your ideas in note form.

2 On your own, jot down notes for another plot. It should be different from both *Home from the Sea* and the one you worked on with your partner.

Activity 10

Choose one of the two plot structures you planned in Activity 9.

a Draft the story whilst remembering:

♦ to have five stages in your story

♦ to keep your story quite short (*Home from the Sea* is less than 400 words long)

♦ not to use too much dialogue (there is very little in *Home from the Sea*).

b When you have finished writing your stories, swap with a partner. Read each other's story and then give feedback on the following:

♦ whether the story uses some of the techniques explored in this unit

♦ whether there are any improvements which could be suggested and discussed.

c The best writers keep re-reading their work as they write, in order to make improvements. Ask yourself if you have:

♦ written an opening that will 'hook' your readers

♦ used some of the ideas and techniques for good openings that you have worked on in this unit

♦ used particular words and phrases for effect like the writers you have studied in this unit

♦ used sentences that contain a lot of detail?

You should also spend time editing your writing. Check spelling and punctuation, and make sure that your sentences will make sense for your reader.

Looking at dialogue

To create an interesting story you will usually use a mixture of:

◆ action – the events of the plot

◆ description – of characters and places, to help readers create pictures in their minds

◆ dialogue – where readers find out important information about characters through what they say.

You have already seen that successful stories need interesting, well shaped plots. They also need interesting characters. In Unit 1 there are 'bad' characters in the extracts from traditional tales:

◆ In *The Abduction of Persephone* (page 9), Hades is the 'bad' character. We see this in his actions – he kidnaps Persephone.

◆ In *Beowulf* (pages 10–13), Grendel is a monstrous character. Readers know this from its actions – it slaughters several people – and from the way it is described – it has 'poisonous yellow eyes', for example.

There are also 'good' characters in the traditional tales in Unit 1:

◆ Beowulf is clearly a hero. We can tell from the description – 'a warrior so tall, so strong' – and from his dialogue – 'Your majesty! ... My name is Beowulf. I have crossed a great sea to come before you, to serve you and to destroy the monster.'

The focus in this unit is on using dialogue to help make characters and situations interesting. Unit 6 explores ways of describing characters.

Dialogue in prose and dramascript

Dramascript is meant to be the basis for something which is acted out and will be seen by an audience.

In **prose**, the writer has to provide all the details for the reader so they can imagine what is happening.

In the following scene, Kevin and Bee are at school. Bee used to be best friends with a girl called Julie, but recently she has joined in with Kevin and his mates when they have teased and bullied Julie. Bee has been feeling a bit guilty about the way she has been treating Julie. There are three parts. Read the scene in groups of three.

p.189

	Kevin	Bee! Have you heard!
	Bee	What?
	Kevin	You haven't heard!
	Bee	Haven't heard what?
	Kevin	About Julie Mills.
	Bee	Yes. Course I have.
	Kevin	Oh. Right.
	Bee	Kev! Wait!
	Kevin	What?
10	**Bee**	Go on. Tell me.
	Kevin	I thought you knew.
	Bee	Tell me!
	Kevin	About Julie's accident?
	Mr Murphy	Come on, Kevin Proctor. Your form's in assembly already.
15	**Kevin**	Sorry, sir.
	Bee	Wait! Kevin! Wait!
	Mr Murphy	And you too, young lady. Have you registered yet?
	Bee	Please, Mr Murphy! Can I just ask … Kevin! Wait!
	Kevin	He'll do us!
20	**Bee**	What happened to Julie?
	Kevin	She got knocked down.
	Mr Murphy	I'm counting, Proctor.
	Kevin	Outside her school.
		She was running away …
25	**Mr Murphy**	Three …
	Bee	I don't believe you, Kevin.
	Mr Murphy	Two …
	Kevin	Cross me heart and hope to die.
30	**Bee**	When? How?
	Kevin	She was taken to …
	Mr Murphy	NOW!
	Kevin	Sorry, sir. Hospital.

*from **How Green You Are!***
by Berlie Doherty

Activity 11 ws ICT

In your group of three, explore this play text further.

1   Look at each line in turn and decide the following:

   a   In what tone of voice would the line be spoken? Which words or phrases need to be emphasised?

   b   What might the character do as they speak the line?

   c   What facial expressions might accompany what they say?

2   Choose *ten* lines from the scene. Copy them down, but also write down a stage direction for how the line is to be spoken and what the character might do. Put your stage direction in brackets, for example:

Mr Murphy	And you too, young lady. Have you registered yet? (*In a stern voice. He leans forward and glares at Bee*)
Bee	Please, Mr Murphy! Can I just ask … Kevin! Wait! (*In a pleading voice. She looks desperate. She grabs Kevin's arm*)
Kevin	He'll do us! (*In a hissed whisper. He turns his face away from Mr Murphy*)

To explore the differences between dialogue in prose and dramascript, read the following dialogue from the opening of a novel called *Goodnight Mr Tom* by Michelle Magorian.

It is 1939 and city children are being moved out to the country, away from the dangers of bombs. It is the job of volunteers called billeting officers to place the children in homes. In this case, a middle-aged female billeting officer has called round to see a man called Thomas Oakley. Thomas Oakley speaks first:

Goodnight Mr Tom

'Yes. What d'you want?'

'I'm the Billeting Officer for this area.'

'Oh yes, and what's that got to do wi' me?'

'Well, Mr, Mr …'

5   'Oakley. Thomas Oakley.'

'Ah, thank you, Mr Oakley. Mr Oakley, with the declaration of war imminent …'

'I knows all that. Git to the point. What d'you want?' (He noticed a small boy at her side.)

'It's him I've come about, I'm on my way to your village hall with the others.'

10   'What others?'

*from **Goodnight Mr Tom** by Michelle Magorian*

Activity 12

The writer uses dialogue to create the characters of Tom and the Billeting Officer and to make the difference between them clear.

1 Tom is given an interesting way of talking. He shortens words and says words in a way that may be considered to be different from usual, 'standard' English. Write down examples of these.

2 Compare how Tom speaks with the way the Billeting Officer speaks. How would you sum up the differences between the two?

In your own story writing you should use similar methods of writing dialogue to make characters different, and interesting. It is quite easy to capture accents and different ways of pronouncing words.

In the novel there is more than just the dialogue. As you read the full version, reflect on what detail is added about these two characters. Is the writing better with the description or without it? Does it make the dialogue easier to follow?

Goodnight Mr Tom

'Yes,' said Tom bluntly, on opening the front door. 'What d'you want?'

A harassed middle-aged woman in a green coat and felt hat stood on his step. He glanced at the armband on her sleeve. She gave him an awkward smile.

'I'm the Billeting Officer for this area,' she began.

5 'Oh yes, and what's that got to do wi' me?'

She flushed slightly. 'Well, Mr, Mr ….'

'Oakley. Thomas Oakley.'

'Ah, thank you, Mr Oakley.' She paused and took a deep breath.

10 'Mr Oakley, with the declaration of war imminent ...'

Tom waved his hand. 'I knows all that. Git to the point. What d'you want?' He noticed a

15 small boy at her side.

'It's him I've come about,' she said. 'I'm on my way to your village hall with the others.'

20 'What others?'

She stepped to one side.

*from **Goodnight Mr Tom**
by Michelle Magorian*

Activity 13

How do the words in **bold** in the table below:

1 help the reader to hear more clearly how the two characters speak?

2 reveal what the characters are like?

Tom	The Billeting Officer
'Yes,' said Tom **bluntly**.	She **flushed slightly**.
'Tom **waved his hand**.'	'She **paused and took a deep breath**.'

Activity 14 ⟨ws⟩

Layout and punctuation are very important when putting speech in a story.

1 Investigate the extract with a partner. Find and list the rules which control how speech is set out. Think about:

  ◆ how words that are spoken are separated from the rest of the story
  ◆ how it is shown that a new person is speaking
  ◆ where speech marks are used
  ◆ where the punctuation goes when closing speech marks
  ◆ where a capital letter is used.

Activity 15

1 When you are writing your own dialogue, avoid using 'he said/she said' all the time. Look up the word 'say' or 'said' in a thesaurus and see how many words (synonyms) there are to choose from. Make your own word bank and refer to it when writing stories.

2 Rewrite these sentences, changing the word 'said' in each case:
   a 'Fire!' he said.
   b 'Stop tickling me!' he said.
   c 'I hate you!' she said.
   d 'If you hate the referee clap your hands,' they said.
   e 'Oh no, not again!' she said.

Sometimes using the word 'said' is enough:

'I'd love a puppy,' she said.

But on other occasions you may wish to add detail:

*'I'd love a puppy,' she said, **gazing longingly in the pet shop window**.*

Notice that the comma after 'said' is used to separate the descriptive detail from the details of speech. The description helps you understand how the girl spoke.

Activity 16

1 Add a short piece of description to each of the following sentences:

   a 'I'm warning you, don't push me too far,' he said,...
   b 'Do I have to tidy my bedroom, Mum?' she said,...
   c 'It's lovely to see you,' she said,...

Activity 17

1 Write a simple conversation between two students who are walking to school on their first day. One of them is shy, saying very little, while the other is outgoing and has a lot to say. Write no more than twenty lines.

Think a little about the situation and the characters. You may like to make a few notes – about the two characters, for example.

Remember to:

◆ make clear who is talking through layout and punctuation
◆ avoid over-using the word 'said'. Use some of the synonyms from your word bank
◆ add descriptive detail in between the actual spoken words.

You could begin like this:

'I'm really looking forward to this, Kev. Do you think we'll have homework tonight?'
'Dunno.'
Karenjit looked sharply at Kevin. 'Are you OK?'
'Sort of.'

2 Once you've written out the conversation, ask yourself the following questions:

◆ Do my two characters speak in different ways?
◆ Does it sound like a real conversation?
◆ Have I avoided overusing 'said'?
◆ Have I given enough information about how things are said?

Make any changes that would improve your writing.

6 Creating people and places

This unit will help you to:
- **describe places and characters in different ways**
- **find different ways of grabbing your reader's attention**
- **choose and use interesting vocabulary**
- **structure paragraphs effectively**
- **plan, draft and present your work.**

Descriptive writing in prose

Zooming in

When you describe something in writing, you have to decide where to begin and end your description. One way to do this is to imagine you are filming a scene and zooming in. Read 'Dark, Dark Tale', which uses this idea.

Once upon a time there was a dark, dark moor.
On the moor there was a dark, dark wood.
In the wood there was a dark, dark house.
At the front of the house there was a dark, dark door.
5 Behind the door there was a dark, dark hall.
In the hall there were some dark, dark stairs.
Up the stairs there was a dark, dark passage.
Across the passage was a dark, dark curtain.
Behind the curtain was a dark, dark room.
10 In the room was a dark, dark cupboard.
In the cupboard was a dark, dark corner.
In the corner was a dark, dark box.
And in the box there was … A MOUSE!

*from **Dark, Dark Tale** by Ruth Brown*

Activity 1 (ws)

Create your own piece of writing where you slowly zoom in on a final surprise.
You could zoom through a city or through forests.
There are different ways of approaching your writing:

- Your version could be very similar to the original, beginning something like:

  Once upon a time there was a cold, wet country.

- It may be better to use your own form of words:

  In the middle of a large grey ocean lay a green and pleasant island.

  On this beautiful island was a deep and dark forest.

63

Detail in prose

When you describe something in writing you also need to include detail and focus your reader on the most important detail. Read the following paragraph:

p.190

Tuck Everlasting

She was unprepared for the homely little house beside the pond, unprepared for the gentle eddies of dust, the silver cobwebs, the mouse who lived – and welcome to him! – in a table drawer. There were only three rooms. The kitchen came first, with an open cabinet where dishes were stacked in perilous towers without the least regard
5   for their varying dimensions. There was an enormous black stove, and a metal sink, and every surface, every wall, was piled and strewn and hung with everything imaginable, from onions to lanterns to wooden spoons to washtubs. And in a corner stood Tuck's forgotten shotgun.

*from **Tuck Everlasting**
by Natalie Babbitt*

Word bank
perilous – dangerous

Activity 2

Work with a partner.

1 Look at the first, third and fourth sentences. List the details – the objects – described by the writer in each sentence.

2 How many details are included in the final sentence of the paragraph? Explore with your partner why you think the writer:
   a made this sentence so short
   b placed it at the *end* of the paragraph?

3 The final short sentence stands out because it begins, unusually, with 'And'. Discuss with your partner why you think the writer decided to place a full stop after 'washtubs' and begin a new sentence with 'And'.

4 The final sentence also stands out because it contrasts with the very long sentence placed immediately before it.

There was an enormous black stove, and a metal sink, and every surface, every wall, was piled and strewn and hung with everything imaginable, from onions to lanterns to wooden spoons to washtubs.

Look at this carefully and with your partner discuss the following:
   a How many different kinds of *repetition* can you find in the long sentence?
   b Why do you think the writer used three verbs – '*piled* and *strewn* and *hung*' – when one or two would have been enough?
   c There are five commas in the long sentence. Why do you think the writer used so many so close to each other? Choose *one* of the commas and write an explanation of why the writer used it in that position.

Another reason why the final sentence stands out is because it contains a detail that is quite different from the previous sentences. A shotgun is not an ordinary household item like the other things mentioned in the paragraph.

Activity 3

Working with a partner, decide on *three* other possible objects that the final sentence could have led up to. Replace 'Tuck's forgotten shotgun' with each of the three different possible items. Each one needs to be something that would cause surprise in the reader but not be so far-fetched as to be completely out of place in this kitchen.

Activity 4

Working on your own, imagine you are visiting a friend's house for the first time. You go into a particular room in their house. Write a description of the contents of the room which ends with a 'zoom in' on a surprising object you see there. You should:

◆ write only five or six sentences

◆ end with a short sentence beginning with 'And'

◆ try to make the second to last sentence long, using some of the same techniques as Natalie Babbitt used in *Tuck Everlasting*

◆ try to make some of the other sentences long, with a number of details included in each.

Before you start, spend a few minutes thinking about the kind of room you wish to describe. It might be one you actually know, or you may wish to invent a particular kind of room – a very untidy one, or a strange one, for example.

Think about the different areas of the room which could contain different items. For example, what is on the floor or by the wall?

You then need to note down some items to include in your description. Think back to Activity 2.1, where you created lists of how many objects were mentioned in the paragraph from *Tuck Everlasting*. That could be a guide to about how many items you need to include in your description.

Remember that the main focus of your writing is *zooming in*.

The walking shot

Sometimes it is best to put yourself in the scene and move around. The following extract is from *Skellig* by David Almond. Michael has just moved house and is exploring the garage. This description shows the importance of focusing on more than one of the senses. Be aware of what you see, hear and feel as Michael moves around.

Skellig

Something little and black scuttled across the floor. The door creaked and cracked for a moment before it was still. Dust poured through the torch beam. Something scratched and scratched in a corner. I tiptoed further in and felt spider webs breaking on my brow. Everything was packed in tight – ancient furniture, kitchen units, rolled-
5   up carpets, pipes and crates and planks. I kept ducking down under the hose-pipes and ropes and kitbags that hung from the roof. More cobwebs snapped on my clothes and skin. The floor was broken and crumbly. I opened a cupboard an inch, shone the torch in and saw a million woodlice scattering away. I peered down into a great stone jar and saw the bones of some little animal that had died in there. Dead
10 bluebottles were everywhere. There were ancient newspapers and magazines. I shone the torch on to one and saw that it came from nearly fifty years ago. I moved so carefully. I was scared every moment that the whole thing was going to collapse. There was dust clogging my throat and nose. I knew they'd be yelling for me soon and I knew I'd better get out. I leaned
15 across a heap of tea chests and shone the torch into the space behind and that's when I saw him.

*from **Skellig** by David Almond*

Activity 5 ⓦ ⓘ

1 List the things Michael:

   a sees   **b** hears   **c** feels.

2 Look more closely at how the writer adds variety to his description and makes it interesting. Here are the first five sentences of the paragraph:

   1 Something little and black scuttled across the floor.

   2 The door creaked and cracked for a moment before it was still.

   3 Dust poured through the torch beam.

   4 Something scratched and scratched in a corner.

   5 I tiptoed further in and felt spider webs breaking on my brow.

   Write down the numbers of the sentences. For each one, note:

   ◆ which of the five senses is being used

   ◆ any repetition of words or letter sounds

   ◆ any words that seem particularly interesting, or unexpected.

3 Now look in detail at some more sentences from the paragraph:

   a David Almond could have written: 'There were dead bluebottles everywhere.' But he chose to write: 'Dead bluebottles were everywhere.' Why do you think he did this?

   b 'I moved so carefully' could simply be 'I moved carefully'. Why did the writer include 'so'?

   c Compare the final sentence with the final sentence of the *Tuck Everlasting* paragraph. How are they similar? How are they different?

4 David Almond chooses words very carefully. Copy this chart, in which the writer's words are in the left-hand column. A more obvious word that he could have chosen is in the middle column. Using a dictionary if necessary, use the right-hand column to explain why you think the writer's choice of words is better.

Writer's choice	Alternative	Explanation
scuttled (line 1)	moved	
tiptoed (line 3)	walked	
snapped (line 6)	broke	
scattering (line 8)	running	
peered (line 8)	looked	

Look at the following pictures. Imagine yourself walking around in one of these scenes.

Activity 6

Choose one of the places in the pictures above. Using what you have learned, write a description based on your chosen location that, like the extract from *Skellig*, ends 'and that's when I saw him'.

Choosing interesting vocabulary

A reader's attention can be gained by structuring descriptions in such a way that they lead up to a surprise, as in *Tuck Everlasting* and *Skellig*. But there are many other ways of grabbing and holding a reader's attention with your writing.

Choosing interesting vocabulary and finding interesting ways of arranging words are also important. In the following extract the writer describes a building from the point of view of an 'ordinary' girl:

Granny was a Buffer Girl

The Cutlers' Hall was in Church Street, near the middle of town. Lights blazed from all its windows. Even from the street outside, with all its bustle of trams and traffic, you could hear the strains
5 of the orchestra, and the babble of voices and laughter. Dorothy, shy, held on to her sister's arm as they went up the steps to the entrance hall. She gazed round at the black and green walls that gleamed like marble, the
10 crystal chandeliers, the glowing polish of the woodwork; at the height of the pillars and the decorated ceiling, and at the broad sweep of the grand staircase that she was going to have
15 to climb up if she was ever going to get near the ballroom.

*from **Granny was a Buffer Girl**
by Berlie Doherty*

Activity 7 ⓦ

1 Instead of writing 'the walls', the writer uses a noun phrase, 'the black and green walls that gleamed like marble'. Identify the noun phrases she uses instead of the simpler 'chandeliers', 'woodwork', 'pillars', 'ceiling' and 'staircase'. Why did the writer choose to use so many noun phrases?

2 Rewrite the long sentence beginning, 'She gazed ...' (lines 8–16) as three or more sentences. When you have finished, try to explain why you think she described all those items in one long sentence, instead of arranging them into two or more sentences.

3 Which words in the description are used by the writer to suggest the large size and grandness of the Hall?

Creating atmosphere

By choosing vocabulary and arranging words imaginatively you can go beyond simple description and create atmosphere in your writing. Read the following description of a small, ruined graveyard:

The Woman in Black

I emerged into a small burial ground. It was enclosed by the remains of a wall, and I stopped in astonishment at the sight. There were perhaps fifty old gravestones, most of them leaning over or completely fallen, covered in patches of greenish-yellow
5 lichen and moss, scoured pale by the salt wind, and stained by years of driven rain. The mounds were grassy, and weed-covered, or else they had disappeared altogether, sunken and slipped down. No names or dates were now decipherable, and the whole place had a decayed and abandoned air.

Ahead, where the wall ended in a heap of dust and rubble, lay the grey water
10 of the estuary. As I stood, wondering, the last light went from the sun, and the wind rose in a gust, and rustled through the grass. Above my head, that unpleasant, snake-necked bird came gliding back towards the ruins, and I saw that its beak was hooked around a fish that writhed and struggled helplessly. I watched the creature alight and, as it did so, it disturbed some of the stones, which toppled and fell out of sight somewhere.

*from **The Woman in Black** by Susan Hill*

Word bank

decipherable – able to be worked out
alight – perch, come to rest

Activity 8

1 The writer has chosen a number of words which suggest how unattractive and run down the place is. List them.

2 Why do you think the writer included the detail of the bird which flies into the burial ground? What effect does her description of the bird have on the reader?

3 In 'the wind rose in a gust, and rustled through the grass', what examples of repeated sounds do you find the writer using? Why might the writer have chosen words for their sounds in this particular section?

Larger than life

Exaggeration can be used to create particular effects and grab readers' attention. This is a particular characteristic of the writing of the nineteenth-century novelist Charles Dickens. Read the following description of a market. It is from Dickens' novel *Oliver Twist*:

A Stunning and Bewildering Scene

Countrymen, butchers, drovers, hawkers, boys, thieves, idlers, and vagabonds of every low grade, were mingled together in a mass; the whistling of drovers, the barking of dogs, the bellowing and plunging of oxen, the bleating of sheep, the grunting and squeaking of pigs; the cries of hawkers, the shouts, oaths, and quarrelling on all sides; the ringing of bells and
5 the roars of voices, that issued from every public-house; the crowding, pushing, driving, beating, whooping, and yelling; the hideous and discordant din that resounded from every corner of the market; and the unwashed, unshaven, squalid, and dirty figures constantly running to and fro, and bursting in and out of the throng; rendered it a stunning and bewildering scene, which quite confounded the senses.

*from **Oliver Twist** by Charles Dickens*

That one long sentence can be divided into two parts:
a a very long list of things (lines 1–8) which
b 'rendered it a stunning and bewildering scene' (lines 8–9).

Word bank
discordant – not in harmony, harsh
rendered it – caused it to be
confounded – confused

Activity 9

1 The writer uses commas (,) and semicolons (;) to separate out the various things in the long list. With a partner, look carefully at where Dickens uses semicolons. Why does he sometimes use them instead of commas?

2 Do you think this is an effective description of a noisy market place? Explain your view.

Activity 10 ICT

Think of a different modern place which is full of people and noise – a school playground perhaps, or a football stadium. Working with a partner, write a description as close to the style of Dickens as you can. Make lists of nouns, verbs and adjectives that you could use. For a school playground you might think of the following:

◆ *nouns:* boys, girls, teachers, footballs, fights, etc.
◆ *verbs:* playing, shouting, ordering, screeching, etc.
◆ *adjectives:* small, large, noisy, running, etc.

The next stage is to try to organise as many things as possible from your lists into one sentence which is as long as you can make it.

Creating characters

The description of characters can be made interesting by using the same kinds of techniques – choosing vocabulary imaginatively and grouping words in unusual ways.

Read the following description of Hagrid from *Harry Potter and the Philosopher's Stone*:

Hagrid

The door was hit with such force that it swung clean off its hinges and with a deafening crash landed flat on the floor.

5   A giant of a man was standing in the doorway. His face was almost completely hidden by a long, shaggy mane of hair and a wild, tangled beard, but you could make out his
10 eyes, glinting like black beetles under all the hair.

    The giant squeezed his way into the hut, stooping so that his head just brushed the ceiling. He bent
15 down, picked up the door and fitted it easily back into its frame.

*from **Harry Potter and the Philosopher's Stone** by J. K. Rowling*

Activity 11 (ICT)

1 What this character *does* helps create a picture of him. However, it is the sentence beginning 'His face was ...', in the second paragraph, which paints the most vivid picture of Hagrid. Which adjectives are used to describe his hair and beard? What aspect of his appearance is being emphasised by repetition?

2 The writer uses a simile – 'glinting like black beetles under all the hair' – to describe Hagrid's eyes. Why do you think she chose that particular comparison?

3 Invent a new character. Write a sentence similar to the one above describing them. Begin with 'His (or her) face was ...' and give them a different kind and colour of hair. (Clearly if your character is female she won't have the beard!) End with a simile to describe the eyes.

This unit will help you to:
- explore and develop ideas in imaginative ways
- experiment with the effects of language
- learn how to use similes
- evaluate the quality of your work.

Developing ideas in poetry
Word association

'Word association' is a game in which someone says a word and the next person has to say a word that is in some way connected with the first word. The next person then has to say a word which has something to do with the second word and so on. For example, you might get a sequence of words such as:

tree > wood > oak > acorn > squirrel > tail > dog > collar

You can use this idea to write poems.

You begin by writing down a word. Then you write down a word that is connected with it, then a word connected with that word and so on. Here's an example beginning with the word 'sky', where all the words are quite tightly connected:

sky ➤ clouds ➤ rain ➤ umbrella

That could lead to a poem of four lines based on those key words. In the first line you would use the word 'sky', in the second line 'clouds', and so on, for example:

Beautiful deep blue **sky**,
Till slate **clouds** bring
Grey sheets of **rain**. Dismal till
Bright multi-coloured **umbrellas** float above the pavements.

Activity 1 ⟨ws⟩

Write your own four-line poem.

Begin by associating four nouns as in the example on the previous page. Then think about each noun in turn, and how you can develop it from the single word to a line of poetry.

There are other ways of writing poems based upon word association. Sometimes it is fun to see how word association can lead you *away from* your starting point.

The purpose of the next activity is to use associations which take you in different directions, although each word must be connected in some way with the word before it. To add interest, there are some other rules:

◆ there must be eight lines
◆ there must be four words in each line
◆ the lines have to rhyme in pairs.

Here is an example:

clock	hands	fingers	nails
hammer	blow	wind	gales
storm	rain	water	sea
fish	chips	potato	pea
green	grass	cow	Jersey
island	country	river	Mersey
Liverpool	city	bank	money
wages	work	bees	honey

Activity 2

Now try your own version of an eight-line poem. You can begin with any noun you choose. The poem works best if all the words you use are nouns.

Rhyming

You will be familiar with **rhyme**, which is the repetition of similar or identical sounds. Where do you find rhyming outside poetry books? How many different uses of rhyme can you think of?

A pair of rhymes is called a **couplet**. Pairing words by sound can be quite easy. But it is more difficult to think of a way of connecting the *ideas* of rhyming words. Choose one of the pairs of rhymes in the box below and see if you can write a couplet. For example, if the pair of words was *bee* and *tea*, you might end up with a couplet such as:

I hope you don't think I'm stealing, bee
When I take your honey for my tea.

◆ frog/dog   ◆ fears/ears   ◆ teacher/creature   ◆ refrigerator/alligator

It's possible to make quite ordinary things seem special by using rhyme. Here is a poem about the kinds of things to be found in a market:

Jamaica Market

Honey, pepper, leaf-green limes,
Pagan fruit whose names are rhymes,
Mangoes, breadfruit, ginger-roots,
Granadillas, bamboo-shoots,
5 Cho-cho, ackees, tangerines,
Lemons, purple Congo-beans,
Sugar, okras, kola-nuts,
Citrons, hairy coconuts,
Fish, tobacco, native hats,
10 Gold bananas, woven mats,
Plantains, wild thyme, pallid leeks
Pigeons with their scarlet beaks,
Oranges and saffron yams,
Baskets, ruby guava jams,
15 Turtles, goat-skins, cinnamon,
Allspice, conch-shells, golden rum.
Black skins, babel – and the sun
That burns all colours into one.

Agnes Maxwell-Hall

Word bank
pallid – pale
saffron – orange/yellow in colour
babel – a scene of noise and confusion

You will see that the lines of 'Jamaica Market' mostly rhyme in pairs. The **rhythm** of the poem, the way your voice goes up and down as you emphasise certain sounds, could be shown like this:

HONey, **pepp**er, **leaf**-green **limes**,
Pagan **fruit** whose **names** are **rhymes**,
Mangoes, **bread**fruit, **ging**er-**roots**,
Granadillas, **bam**boo-**shoots**,

Activity 3 ICT

Working with a partner, say the poem out loud to each other. Read alternate lines, trying to capture the rhythm.

Syllables are parts of words. 'Granadillas' has four syllables: gran – a – dill – as. All the lines have seven syllables in them and in each line they can be put into a pattern like the one shown above. But the last line is different:

That burns all colours into one.

In what ways is it different? Can you and your partner provide any explanation for that?

Activity 4

'Jamaica Market' consists mainly of the names of different kinds of food. These are nouns. But there are also a lot of adjectives. Look at these five examples of adjectives taken from the poem. Select *three* and explore why you feel the writer has chosen that particular adjective. The first one has been analysed for you.

- ◆ Gold bananas
- ◆ leaf-green limes
- ◆ pallid leeks
- ◆ scarlet beaks
- ◆ saffron yams.

'Gold bananas' is slightly unusual. You might expect 'Yellow bananas'. What the poet has written is much better for at least two reasons. First, 'Yellow bananas' is a bit like 'wet rain' or 'white snow' – it is boringly obvious. Second, 'Gold' makes the bananas sound special, like a precious metal, and that's what she seems to be doing in the poem – making ordinary things seem special.

Activity 5

Working with a partner, write your own poem based on a list of nouns like the poem 'Jamaica Market'. You could try writing about a local market, or a supermarket, or the street, a school, the city – anywhere you like.
If you feel confident you could try to work the lines of your poem into the same strong rhythm as 'Jamaica Market'. Each line should contain seven syllables.
Try to write at least ten lines. Draft your poem first.

Drafting poems

Drafting doesn't have to mean writing and rewriting the whole poem.

The first planning stage or draft of your poem could be a simple list of the words you would like to use – associated words. The second stage might be to group the words as they rhyme and to think of other rhyming words. For example, if you were going to write a poem based on a school you could use a chart like this:

First list of words	Possible rhymes	Ideas for added detail (colour, sound, texture)
blackboard	bored	'chalky' board
call	football	words for sounds: 'piercing call' 'shouting boys playing football'?
exercise books	teachers' stern looks	
head	bike shed	
corridor	classroom door	
detention	students' attention	

The next stage is to begin working on a pair of lines, trying to achieve something that works well. The words in the chart above might lead to a poem beginning:

Bright displays in corridors
Posters stuck on classroom doors.

You can then carry on building up the poem in this way.

Patterns of rhyme and rhythm

Here is another poem with a strong pattern of rhyme and rhythm.
Read it with a partner and then work on the activities on page 80.

The Sound Collector

A stranger called this morning
Dressed all in black and grey
Put every sound into a bag
And carried them away.

5 The whistling of the kettle
The turning of the lock
The purring of the kitten
The ticking of the clock

The popping of the toaster
10 The crunching of the flakes
When you spread the marmalade
The scraping noise it makes

The hissing of the frying-pan
The ticking of the grill
15 The bubbling of the bathtub
As it starts to fill

The drumming of the raindrops
On the window-pane
When you do the washing-up
20 The gurgle of the drain

The crying of the baby
The squeaking of the chair
The swishing of the curtain
The creaking of the stair

25 A stranger called this morning
He didn't leave his name
Left us only silence
Life will never be the same.

Roger McGough

Here are two different patterns of the beats (or stressed syllables) in 'The Sound Collector', using the same method as for 'Jamaica Market' on page 77. Discuss each pattern with your partner and decide which one sounds best and makes most sense.

1 The **whist**ling **of** the **kett**le
The **turn**ing **of** the **lock**
The **purr**ing **of** the **kitt**en
The **tick**ing **of** the **clock**

2 The **whist**ling of the **kett**le
The **turn**ing of the **lock**
The **purr**ing of the **kitt**en
The **tick**ing of the **clock**

Activity 6 ICT

1 Using the same pattern as Roger McGough, try to write your own poem about sounds. You could write about school sounds, city sounds, a sports hall, a railway station; or you could imagine that the Sound Collector called at your house in the evening, when the sounds would be different.

Use the same approach to planning and drafting as you did on page 78. Begin with simple lists, next think of possible rhymes, then group ideas together, and finally try to introduce the same rhythm as Roger McGough.

2 Whereas 'Jamaica Market' is based on nouns, 'The Sound Collector' is largely based on an interesting selection of verbs describing sounds. It uses a repeated pattern:

The (verb, *perhaps ending with 'ing'*) of the (noun *responsible for the sound*)

In a poem about the city, you might write lines like:

The **rumble** of the **traffic**
The **clatter** of the **train**
The **screeching** of the **brakes**
The **hooting** of the **horns**

The next stage would be to think about possible rhymes. For example, 'The **clatter** of the **train**' could be rhymed with something else heard in cities: 'The **patter** of the **rain**'.

Then you would need to choose four lines and arrange them so that the second line rhymes with the fourth line.

Experimenting with words

When you rhyme, you are connecting different words because they sound similar. Sometimes rhyming words have obvious connections, like *star* and *far*, *frown* and *down*. Sometimes they seem to be opposites, like *sad* and *glad*, *light* and *night*. They may seem to have no connection at all but poets often bring ideas together in quite entertaining ways:

Alligator

From Sydney Zoo
An Alligator
Was put on board
A flying freighter.
5 He ate the pilot
And the navigator
Then asked for more,
With mashed potater.

Spike Milligan

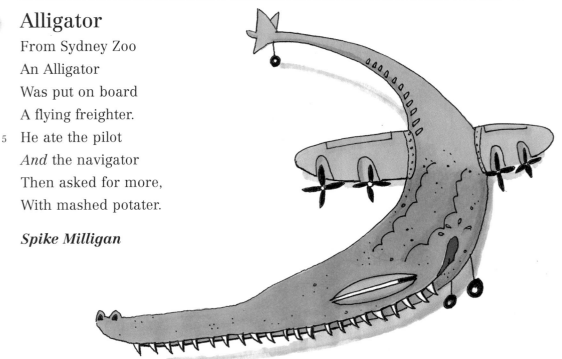

Spike Milligan uses four rhyming words as the basis for his poem. He's 'cheated' a little with one. Which one?

Activity 7

1 Try writing your own poem based on four rhyming words as in the poem above. For practice, you could make a poem out of one of the following sets of four rhymes:

> footballer / taller / smaller / brawler
> lorry / worry / quarry / sorry

If you can, come up with your own four rhyming words.

2 When you have finished your poem, share it with a partner. Discuss your poem and how good it is. In particular comment on the rhymes: do they make your poem enjoyable or does it seem as if you have been forced to write things that sound awkward because of the rhymes? If so, in what way are you able to change your poem for the better?

Making comparisons

Poets make connections in other ways. Very often they describe things by comparing them with something else. Look at the following comparisons and see if you can work out what is being described. Match each poem to the correct letter.

1 A drifting, fringed, lampshade
in the dusk
of the deep.

Stewart Henderson

2 … sudden fiery flowers
That burst upon the night.

James Reeves

3 Grazing down on the carpet pasture:
Cow with electric bones.

Kit Wright

4 Chinese characters
In the lower sky …

Douglas Dunn

5 He duels with himself and woos his
women customers …

Craig Raine

6 who carries his pregnant belly
in the hammock of his leotard

like a melon wedged in a shopping-bag …

Christopher Reid

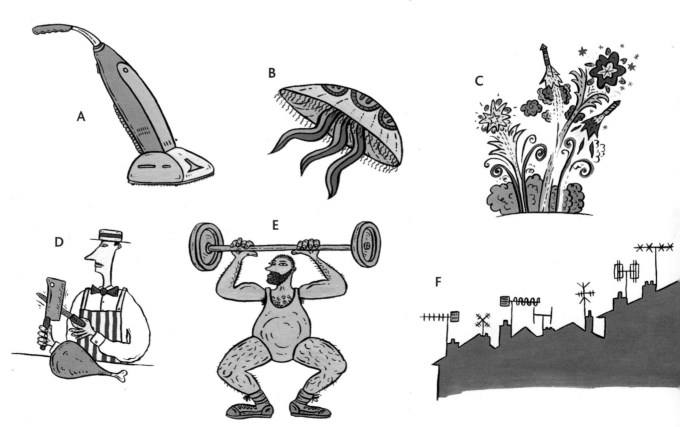

Similes

When poets compare two things using the words 'like' or 'as', they are using what is called a **simile**. Similes can be very simple or very complicated. By reading the following **stanzas** or verses from a long poem written in the nineteenth century, you may be able to revise or extend what you already know about similes.

The skipper of a sailing ship called the *Hesperus* has taken his daughter on a voyage, but the ship sails into trouble. This is the section that describes the fate of the ship.

As you read, look for similes. How many can you count?

The Wreck of the *Hesperus*

And fast through the midnight dark and drear,
    Through the whistling sleet and snow,
Like a sheeted ghost, the vessel swept
    Towards the reef of Norman's Woe.

5 And ever the fitful gusts between
    A sound came from the land;
It was the sound of the trampling surf,
    On the rocks and the hard sea-sand.

The breakers were right beneath her bows,
10   She drifted a dreary wreck,
And a whooping billow swept the crew
    Like icicles from her deck.

She struck where the white and fleecy waves
    Looked soft as carded wool,
15 But the cruel rocks, they gored her side
    Like the horns of an angry bull.

Her rattling shrouds, all sheathed in ice,
    With the masts went by the board;
Like a vessel of glass, she stove and sank,
20   Ho! Ho! The breakers roared!

*from **The Wreck of the Hesperus** by
Henry Wadsworth Longfellow*

Word bank
drear – gloomy
carded – combed
shrouds – ropes that keep a mast upright
sheathed – coated
stove – broke up

83

Activity 8 WS ICT

1 **a** Write down *three* of the similes that you found in the stanzas from 'The Wreck of the *Hesperus*'.

 b Write an explanation of each one. What picture is the writer painting for you? You may be able to produce a sketch of them. You could approach this by filling in a chart like this:

Simile	Explanation	Sketch
... the cruel rocks, they gored her side Like the horns of an angry bull.	The rocks are described as cruel because they are like a vicious bull attacking the helpless ship. Their sharp edges are like a bull's horns, sharp and dangerous. It almost sounds as if the rocks are charging forward to attack the ship. The ship sounds as if it is an innocent victim – a helpless woman.	

From this example you can see that some similes have more levels of meaning than you might think at first. Your previous work on word association (pages 74–75) should show you that words can be connected in different ways.

2 Try writing descriptions of the following, using similes. Use the word 'like' in your descriptions.

> ◆ a car ◆ a school bell ◆ a wasp ◆ an electric kettle ◆ a baby ◆ night ◆ clouds.

You can write longer poems based on similes. Here's a poem about something which the writer compares with lots of other things:

Like the white curls from a gigantic beard
Drifting across the barber's shop floor
In the breeze from the open door;
Like the broken parts of the ice floe
5 Afloat on the blue of the ocean,
Drifting southward from the Pole;
Like a heavily laden treasure fleet
In a light wind on a calm sea,
Hardly moving with all sails set;
10 Like suds of foam from a waterfall
That lathers the rocks at its foot,
Gliding over a tranquil pool;
Like wool from a fleece,
Like smoke from a fire,
15 Like islands in the sky.

Stanley Cook

Look at page 85 if you need help working out what the poem is about.

Activity 9 (WS) (ICT)

Write your own simile poem. You will need to spend some time thinking about what to describe and then what you could compare it to. It would be a good idea to make a spider diagram to help you draft your ideas. For example, if you wanted to describe a football crowd you might draft out something like this:

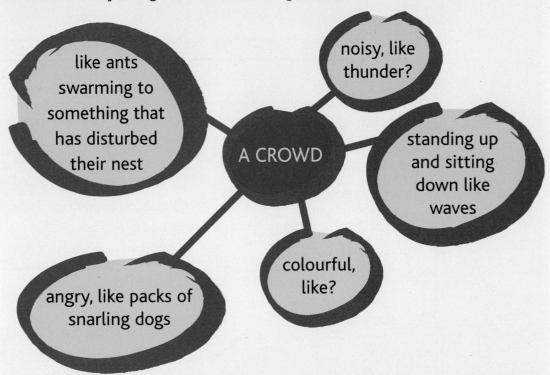

Once you've planned a few ideas, you could start to think about which ones are best and then what the best order for them would be. You could call your poem 'Simile Poem' or, if you want to help the reader guess, give it the name of whatever it is you are describing.

When you have finished your simile poem, share it with a partner. Discuss the following with them:

◆ **How effective your poem is**
  – does it create pictures that interest a reader?
  – do the comparisons go beyond the obvious senses of sight and hearing?
  – is it organised in an effective way?

◆ **How you approached it**
  – explain how you thought of ideas and then arranged them in the best way.

Finally, discuss whether any changes could be made to the poem that might make it even better.

Stanley Cook's poem on page 84 is about clouds.

Write a short story.

A magazine is looking for short stories written by young people for young people. Each week it has a theme. The theme for this week is 'Strange Places'. It is hoping to receive interesting stories. These are the notes for guidance it sends out:

OUR READERS LIKE short interesting stories which have:

- ⊚ clearly described settings
- ⊚ convincing characters
- ⊚ good plots.

It is the policy of the magazine to encourage young writers to use a style of writing in which:

- ⊚ vocabulary is used in interesting and imaginative ways
- ⊚ there is a variety of sentence styles.

Your starting point should be that a character or group of characters is in one of the following settings:

- ⊚ stranded on a distant planet
- ⊚ stranded on a small island
- ⊚ visiting a new city
- ⊚ lost in a forest
- ⊚ in the place you live now but one hundred years in the future.

Tips

We suggest you **plan your story** first, as it is very important that it has a **clear structure**. In particular we would recommend that you try extra hard to **'hook' your readers** in an especially well written opening.

Our readers tend to like a mix of **description**, **action** and **dialogue**.

We have found that successful stories contain **well chosen vocabulary**, a **mixture of kinds of sentence**, and **imaginative forms of expressions**: we have received letters of praise for the **'poetic' touch** of some of our writers.

We would like to receive:

A your plot outline

B your finished story.

Section C ◆ Reading non-fiction and media
Introduction

Non-fiction texts are not poems, stories, novels or plays. They are not made up. There is a huge range of non-fiction texts. These include letters, diaries, leaflets, articles and adverts. Media is the name given to types of communication that reach large numbers of people. Some examples of media are television, radio, the Internet and newspapers.

In Year 6 you will have explored the different styles and features of a range of non-fiction texts, including reviews, leaflets and reports. You will also have investigated how texts are written and presented in different ways to communicate well with their readers.

You will be building on these skills in the three units of work in this section.

In Unit 9, *Evaluating presentation*, you will look at a range of forms of non-fiction texts and explore how information can be organised. You will identify widely-used presentational features and consider how they affect the reader.

In Unit 10, *Investigating the media*, you will assess how media texts are geared to purpose and audience. You will discover how meaning can be created through print and images and will experiment with selecting stories for a newspaper front page.

In Unit 11, *Reading for different purposes*, you will explore different ways of reading for different purposes. By focusing on single words and phrases you will learn to read between the lines and to draw careful conclusions.

Unit 12 tests you on the skills you will develop as you work carefully through the three units.

This unit will help you to:

- ◆ appreciate the range of forms of non-fiction texts
- ◆ understand how information can be organised
- ◆ recognise the cues to start a new paragraph
- ◆ recognise the use of presentational features
- ◆ consider how presentational features affect the reader.

What are non-fiction texts?

What do you know about non-fiction texts? Copy and add to this map.

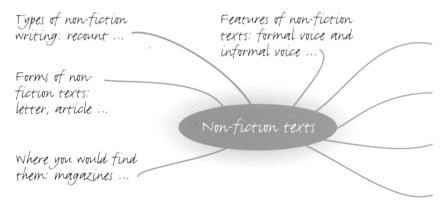

Types of non-fiction writing: recount ...

Features of non-fiction texts: formal voice and informal voice ...

Forms of non-fiction texts: letter, article ...

Non-fiction texts

Where you would find them: magazines ...

Non-fiction texts are not poems, stories, novels or plays. They are not made up. You may be familiar with different types of non-fiction writing: report, recount, explanation, instruction, persuasion and discursive. These types can take many different **forms**. Each form has particular features – things that are special to it.

Activity 1 (WS)

You are going to think about the forms and features of non-fiction texts.

1 On the opposite page are five non-fiction texts, A–E. Study them and identify their forms and *three* features of each form. Copy and complete the chart below. Text A has been done for you.

Text	Form	Features
A	Letter	◆ address and date in top right-hand corner ◆ starts with 'Dear Supporter' ◆ ideas set out in paragraphs
B		

2 Look around your classroom. List the forms of non-fiction texts you can see. What are the features of these forms?

A

NSPCC
Cruelty to children must stop. FULL STOP.

National Society for the Prevention
of Cruelty to Children

42 Curtain Road
London EC2A 3NH
Telephone: 020-7825 2505

20th March 2001

Dear Supporter,

I am writing to you at a momentous time in our history.

The NSPCC is facing a greater challenge than any it has faced before, by launching a national campaign to *put a final full stop to child abuse*.

C

SCHOOL TERM POOL PROGRAMME

MONDAY	TUESDAY	WEDNESDAY
Day Break Dip Lane Swimming 7.30am – 8.30am	Day Break Dip Lane Swimming 7.00am – 8.30am	Day Break Dip Lane Swimming* 7.30am – 8.30am
Public Swim 8.30am – 9.30am	Adult Lessons 8.30am – 9.30am	Public Swim 8.30am – 9.15am
Schools 9.30am – 11.45am	Schools 9.30am – 12.00pm	Schools 9.15am – 12.00pm
Aquahealth 11.45am – 12.45pm	Lunch Break Dip Lane Swimming 12.00pm – 1.30pm	Lunch Break Dip Lane Swimming 12.00pm – 1.30pm
Lunch Break Dip Lane Swimming 12.45pm – 2.30pm	50+ & Parent and Tot 1.30pm – 2.30pm	Aquacise 1.30pm – 2.30pm

Plain Memo

Urgent   FILE PRINT SAVE DELETE ENCL CLIP SPELL RECEIPT SEND

TO: Jack
CC:

Subject: Hiya

Hi. How R U? I've had txts from loadsa ppl 2day. :) Wot R U doing 2moro? Txt me back B4 6, OK? NE Way, g2g now, cya. Lizzi

D

B

CHINESE PUZZLE OVER WILLIAM THE FISH

WILLIAM the resident fish at Florence Fan's Chinese restaurant is a mouthy sort.

Whenever Florence, pictured below, approaches his tank he looks ready to bite her head off. And he's the same with her women customers – one gaze at a female and he goes into a rage, kicking up the sand in his aquarium.

But it's a different story when a man approaches his tank at a Birmingham restaurant. William, a giant gourami from South-East Asia, calms down and seems perfectly content, as though he were one of the lads.

Florence can't figure out the reason for his odd behaviour, but suspects he's just an old sexist with a sweet and sour personality.

E

◼ BEARS' BEANFEAST ◼

Serves 4

INGREDIENTS	YOU WILL NEED
1 large onion	knife, for chopping
1 teaspoon corn oil	chopping board
8 chipolata sausages	teaspoon
1 × 450 g (1 lb) can baked beans	frying pan
75 g (3 oz) frozen mixed vegetables	fish slice
2 slices processed Cheddar cheese	plate
	wooden spoon
	can opener
	tiny cocktail cutter

Preparation time: 15 minutes
Cooking time: 25 minutes

1. Peel and chop the onion and put it to one side.
2. Put the oil into a frying pan and heat it gently. Add the sausages and cook gently for about 10 minutes, turning frequently with a fish slice until the sausages are golden brown all over.
3. Transfer the sausages to a plate with the fish slice. Fry the chopped onion in the frying pan for 5 minutes, stirring often with the wooden spoon.
4. Carefully drain off the oil from the pan. Add the baked beans and frozen mixed vegetables and stir well.

Presenting information

In Year 7 you will come across many different non-fiction textbooks. The presentation of these books will be affected by:

◆ the subject you are studying   ◆ the information being presented.

You will, however, note many similarities between them. As you use the textbooks, think about why the presentational features have been used.

Activity 2 WS ICT

Read this extract from a food technology textbook. The presentational features have been labelled for you. Copy and complete this chart, matching each feature to its possible purposes.

Purpose	Presentational feature (letter)
to divide the information up clearly	A C D F
to tell you what the chapter is about	
to tell you what a part of the chapter is about	
to organise a series of separate points	
to make the main points stand out	
to help the reader visualise what is being said	

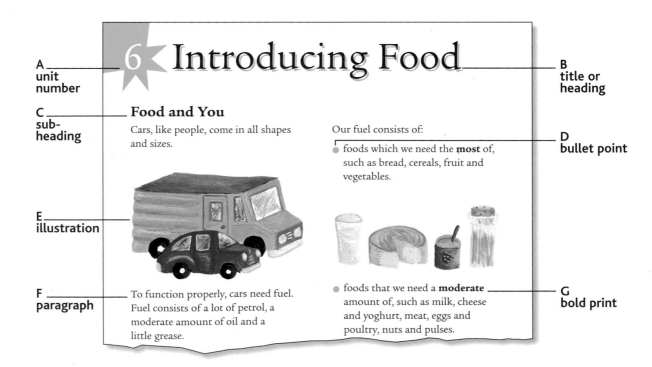

A
unit
number

B
title or
heading

C
sub-
heading

D
bullet point

E
illustration

F
paragraph

G
bold print

6 **Introducing Food**

Food and You

Cars, like people, come in all shapes and sizes.

To function properly, cars need fuel. Fuel consists of a lot of petrol, a moderate amount of oil and a little grease.

Our fuel consists of:

● foods which we need the **most** of, such as bread, cereals, fruit and vegetables.

● foods that we need a **moderate** amount of, such as milk, cheese and yoghurt, meat, eggs and poultry, nuts and pulses.

This extract is taken from a geography textbook. Read it carefully and find these presentational features:

◆ heading ◆ sub-heading ◆ bold print ◆ photographs.

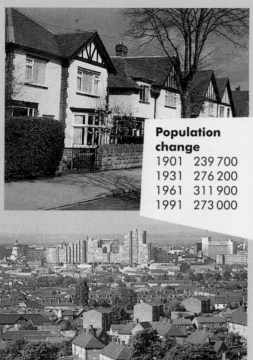

Places For People

Places For People

Nottingham, UK, 2

In the twentieth century large housing estates were built on the edge of Nottingham. Old housing areas were either improved, or demolished and rebuilt. Some old industries moved out of the city to new sites where there was more space.

Population change
1901   239 700
1931   276 200
1961   311 900
1991   273 000

Activity 3 ⓒ

1 A caption is a brief explanation that tells you something about a picture. Match these captions to the photographs in the extract:

   a Some old industries have moved to the edge of the city.

   b Twentieth-century houses south of the river.

   c Good access to Nottingham.

   d A re-developed housing area near the city centre.

2 Look at the chart. What does it tell you about:

   a the population in 1961

   b the differences in population between 1901 and 1991?

3 Think about why and when writers use charts to give information. Develop your thoughts around:

   ◆ the space they take up

   ◆ the use of facts and figures

   ◆ the ways they help the reader make comparisons.

4 Make a list of *five* points which explain why and when writers might use charts.

Charts, diagrams, illustrations and photographs play an important part in the presentation of information. Sometimes, as you have just seen, a picture has a caption to explain it. At other times, writers use labels to tell you more.

Read this extract from a science textbook:

Using Bunsen Burners

Heating Liquids

tongs

Never use this flame on liquids.

Hold the test tube at a slant. Never point it towards anyone. Shake it gently all the time.

liquid: test tube 1/5 full

200°C

400°C

500°C

This flame will make things black and sooty.

This flame is used most often.

This flame is used to heat things strongly.

air hole closed

air hole just open

air hole open

(a) Easily seen flame

(b) Normal flame

(c) Very hot flame

Activity 4 ICT

1 What do you learn from the diagram and labels about the following:
   a how to get different flames
   b the temperature differences between the flames
   c the effects of the different flames
   d how to hold a test tube
   e the things you should *not* do?

2 Suppose the writer had decided to explain all this information *without* using a labelled diagram. Try to write the explanation that would be needed.

3 List the advantages of using a labelled diagram to explain this information. Are there any disadvantages? If so, what are they?

Paragraphs

A writer can organise information by using **paragraphs**. A new paragraph can be shown in one of two ways:

◆ indenting the first word so that it starts a little way in from the margin
◆ leaving a line space between two paragraphs.

Find examples of both methods in this textbook.

It is important to understand *why* and *how* writers use paragraphs, and to use them in your own writing. Read these opening paragraphs from a chapter in a history book about the Vikings. Think and, with a partner, talk about the questions that surround the text.

Would it make sense if this paragraph were placed second or third?

How do the first four words link with paragraph 1?

What, according to the opening sentence, is this paragraph about?

What four more details are you given about the chieftains?

Could it be placed first or third?

How does this paragraph link with paragraphs 1 and 2? Could it be placed first or second?

Viking society was clearly divided into classes. At the top of the social structure were the royal families. Viking kings were brave warriors who led their men in battle, and protected their people from pirates and invaders. They usually had the final say in matters of law, and they acted as religious leaders.

Just below the kings were the chieftains or nobles, who were landowners and warriors. These were the fierce Vikings who raided abroad and led the armies that terrorised much of western Europe in the ninth and tenth centuries. In early Viking times, many powerful chieftains had their own large war bands. They controlled vast areas of Scandinavia in almost complete independence.

As time passed the kings grew more successful in controlling the chieftains. They took away many of the chieftains' powers and gradually unified their lands under royal sovereignty, or control.

What do you think is the subject of this chapter?

Why has the writer decided to start with the kings?

Who are 'They'?

Who are 'These'?

How do the first three words move things on?

Who are 'They?'

How does the second sentence help to explain the first?

*from **The Vikings** by Anne Pearson*

Activity 5 🖳

1 In pairs, list what you have worked out about:

◆ the opening sentence of a paragraph
◆ how the rest of the paragraph supports the opening sentence
◆ the use of pronouns
◆ the ways links are made between paragraphs
◆ the order in which paragraphs are placed.

2 Think about a situation where someone is in charge of others, for example a parent and children, or a manager and team. Write three paragraphs about them.

Your first paragraph should be about the person in charge. Your second paragraph should be about the people below them. Your third paragraph should show the link between them.

The first sentence of each paragraph should:

◆ make clear what it is to be about
◆ provide a link with the previous paragraph.

Use the example on the previous page as a model for your writing.

Activity 6 ⓦⓢ

This text is also about Vikings. The paragraphs are not in their correct order.

1 Identify the main topic of each paragraph.

2 Using the letters only, organise the paragraphs in a logical order. For each letter, explain why you have chosen to put it in that position. For example:

A *I have placed this (first/second/third/fourth) because ...*

> **A** Most new babies were welcomed into the family. They were given a name, sprinkled with water, and then lifted on to their father's knee as a sign of acceptance into the family. Children were given presents to mark the occasion, and later received another one when they cut their first tooth.
>
> **B** Viking children were the pride of their parents. Because life was so hard, many children probably died before they reached adulthood. Those who did survive must have been very strong and independent.
>
> **C** As soon as children were old enough, their parents began to teach them all they knew. Girls were taught how to spin and weave by their mothers, and boys went out in fishing boats with their fathers. Both worked on the family farm. They took the pigs to market, scared birds away from the crops, and helped at home with baking, smoking fish, making butter and many other household tasks.
>
> **D** Although there was an ancient law that allowed babies to be killed, this happened very rarely. Only those babies that did not look as if they could survive the rigours of Viking life, or babies born when there was a famine, were left outside to die.
>
> *from **The Vikings** by Anne Pearson*

3 Could you have chosen another order that would also have made sense? If so, explain it.

4 In the original text, paragraph C is fourth. Here is the paragraph which follows it. Read it carefully. The first sentence has been removed.

Think about how it might be linked to paragraph C. Write *two* possible opening sentences that would make the link clear.

Your sentence should link the paragraphs here.

> In the cold northern winters they skated on icy ponds, wearing shoes with bone skates attached. We know they had balls and other wooden and fabric toys, although few of these have survived.

Use of colour

Drawings and photographs are often used in non-fiction texts to illustrate ideas and to add interest. Colours are used because they can directly affect the way the reader responds to a text. Certain colours tend to be linked with particular moods, ideas and objects. Take the colour black:

night–evil–ghosts –graveyards

death–funerals

tar on roads– coal–blackbird– raven–pitch black

a black mood– depressed–angry– cross–dangerous– black hole

witches–cats– cauldrons

Think about these colours:

Map your own ideas to show what *one* of these colours suggests to you.

Activity 7 WS ICT

Study the Sea Life leaflet on the opposite page. Think about its presentation, in particular:

◆ the information you are given

◆ how you are given it.

1 Write two or three sentences about each of the following:
   a the colours used and the reasons for these
   b the differences in type and size of print and the reasons for these
   c what the photographs show and the impressions they give
   d the map and its usefulness
   e other presentational features you think are important.

2 a Identify the main topic of the first paragraph.
   b Explain how the information in this paragraph links to the topic.

3 This leaflet was written and designed to attract people to the Sea Life Centre. With a partner, talk about:

   ◆ the things you think work well in it
   ◆ the things you think do *not* work well in it
   ◆ any extra information you would like to have
   ◆ whether or not it makes you want to go there, and why.

4 Think about the range of presentational features you have considered in this unit. List those you might use when writing each of the following:
   a a set of instructions on how to play a game
   b an advertisement for a charity event
   c a report on a school football match
   d a research project on volcanoes.

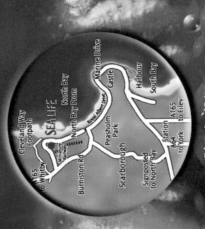

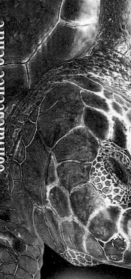

This unit will help you to:
- ◆ identify how media texts are matched to purpose and audience
- ◆ recognise how print and images combine to create meaning
- ◆ think about how news is selected
- ◆ present findings fairly and give a personal view
- ◆ write reflectively about a media text.

What are the media?

The **media** is the name given to types of communication that reach large numbers of people. Each type is known as a medium. The media are very powerful and they are all around you.

Activity 1 ⓌS

You already know a great deal about the media. Copy and develop the map below further and in new directions.

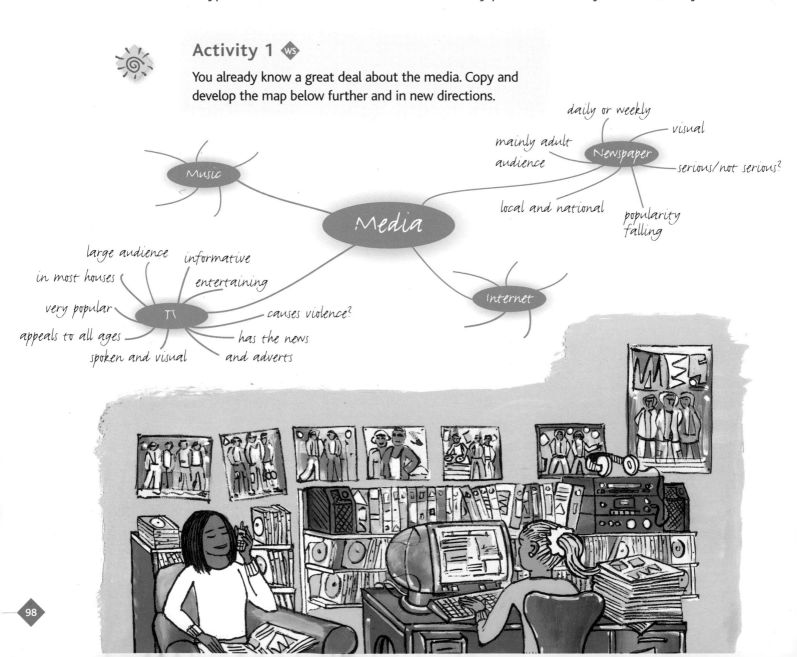

Purpose and audience

Those who design and write media texts always have in mind:

◆ **a particular purpose**: this is their reason for doing it; they might have more than one purpose in mind;

◆ **a particular audience**: this is the intended reader, listener or viewer; they might have more than one audience in mind.

Activity 2 ⟨WS⟩ ⟨ICT⟩

Copy and complete this chart by suggesting the intended purpose(s) and audience(s) of these media texts:

Media text	Intended purpose(s)	Intended audience(s)
Front page headline of newspaper	◆ to attract attention ◆ to interest ◆ to give information	◆ adults who buy newspapers
Breakfast TV		
Billboard advert for chocolate	◆ to attract attention ◆ to persuade people to buy the product	
Teenage magazine		◆ teenagers ◆ usually girls
TV late evening news		
A young child's story-book		◆ the child who will read it ◆ the adult who will buy it

To be effective the media text needs to focus on its purpose(s) and target its audience(s). The text usually contains clues to help you identify its purpose and audience. These include:

◆ what it's about   ◆ the colours used

◆ the images used   ◆ the formal or informal style of writing.

Activity 3 ⟨ICT⟩

1 Look at and read the website home pages on the next page. Copy and complete this chart.

Home page	Clues about purpose	What it's trying to do	Clues about audience	Who it's aimed at
Leeds United				
mykindaplace.com				

2 List *four* similarities and *four* differences between the home pages.

3 Discuss:
  a how effective you think these home pages are
  b how Leeds United and mykindaplace.com could measure their success.

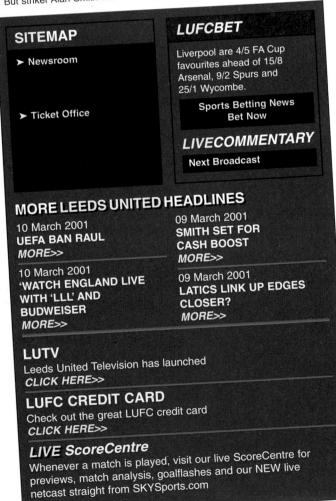

Advertising

You probably noticed that both the home pages you have just looked at carried advertising.
Advertising plays an important part in the media. There are advertisements on television, the
radio, at the cinema, in newspapers and magazines, on billboards and public transport and on
the Internet. The purpose of most advertisements is to sell an idea or a product. To do this,
advertisers use words and images that target their audiences.

Activity 4 (WS)

1   Look at and read The Guide Association advertisement, and then answer the
    questions that surround it.

What is
strange
about the
heading?

Who is its
intended
audience?

What is
the effect
of the use of
imperatives?

What is the purpose of
this advertisement?

How and
why does
the writer
use
repetition?

What does this
picture tell you
about these girls?

How could
The Guide
Association
measure its
success?

2   How successful or otherwise do you think this advertisement would be?
    Give *three* reasons for your answer.

Print and images together

Images are widely used in media texts. The same image can be used to show very different things. Often it is the caption, the short explanation by the picture, which gives it its meaning. Look at this picture. Talk about how these two captions create a different meaning for the same photograph.

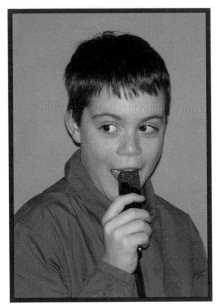

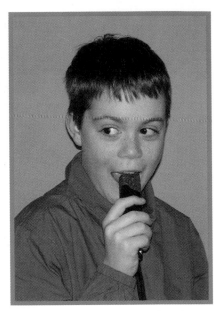

For John the road to heart disease starts early

For energy and vitality John makes the right choice

The same photograph could be used in an advertising campaign with the caption 'Fabulous, scrumptious delight – all in one bar'. How does this caption give it another very different meaning?

In choosing a caption or slogan, you are giving the picture its meaning. This technique, of fixing the meaning of a picture by the words you place with it, is known as **anchoring**.

Activity 5 ICT

In groups, think up as many different captions as you can for these two photographs.

Both of these photographs are to be used in:

◆ a serious news article ◆ an advertisement.

Choose the best caption and slogan for each picture. Explain how they give the picture a different meaning.

The selection of news

Newspapers claim to deal with the news. But what is news?

In pairs or groups, talk about possible answers to the questions below. Record your ideas in note form if you want to use them in a wider discussion.

- ◆ What is news?
- ◆ Who decides what news to print?
- ◆ What makes some stories more newsworthy than others?

- ◆ Where does news come from?
- ◆ Is most news bad news?
- ◆ Do I have a choice about the news I get?

Many things happen in the world, or even in one country, in a day. Someone needs to decide what to select and what to reject. In a newspaper that person is the **editor**.

There are two different kinds of national newspapers in the UK:

Broadsheets – these are newspapers printed on large sheets of paper, e.g. *The Times*, the *Guardian*. They are thought to deal with more serious issues.

Tabloids – these are newspapers printed on smaller sheets of paper, e.g. the *Sun*, the *Mirror*. They are thought to deal with less serious issues.

Activity 6

You are part of an editorial group which considers new stories for the editor. Your job is to provide a balanced view about how newsworthy different stories are.

On the next page are the headlines and summaries of six possible stories. Select the *three* stories which you think should make the front page.

In pairs or groups, follow these stages to make your selection:

1   Decide whether you are working for a broadsheet or a tabloid newspaper.

2   What do you think makes a good front page? Use these words as prompts for your thinking:

- ◆ sensational
- ◆ eye-catching
- ◆ variety
- ◆ interesting
- ◆ national
- ◆ appealing
- ◆ serious
- ◆ disastrous
- ◆ contrast
- ◆ range.

Then list *four* qualities of a good front page.

WS **3** For all six stories give *at least one* reason why:

◆ you might want it on the front page   ◆ you might not want it on the front page.

Write your reasons on a chart like this:

Story	Reasons for selection	Reasons against selection
A		

4 Look at your 'Reasons for selection' column. Which reason do you think is most important when considering the front page of a newspaper? Why?

Place the stories in order, with the one you most want on the front page numbered 1 and the one you least want numbered 6.

5 The story you have as 1 will be your lead story. What photograph would you like to go with it? What will its caption be? Imagine how this story will look. Will it be a success? Why?

A

Fat Facts – Child Health Scare

Results of a recent survey – concern about health issues – advice to parents

B

Woman gives birth to quintuplets

Five children born to woman in New Zealand – three boys and two girls – all babies have been taken off ventilators and are doing well

C

40 DIE IN TRAIN CRASH

Train crash in India has resulted in many deaths and casualties – cause as yet unknown

D

AMAZING achievement of round-world yachtswoman

Twenty-four-year-old arrives on safe soil after sailing single-handed around the world – exhausted but delighted

E

£ drops in value for third week running

Concern growing in the city as pound continues to fall – Chancellor to hold an urgent meeting at Downing Street

F

TEN MILLION watch fate of final five

Popular real-life drama programme attracted record audiences when it revealed what happened to the final five island inhabitants

Activity 7 WS

The editor of the paper is very busy and has asked you to present your ideas for the front page in writing. You need to present the information and arguments clearly so that she can make the final decision later. Follow these stages:

1 Organise your writing into *three* paragraphs.

Paragraph 1 is your introduction. It should:

- ◆ state clearly what you are writing about
- ◆ outline the qualities of a good front page (use your list from Activity 6.2, page 103).

In Paragraph 2 you should write about each of the six articles. Use your chart from Activity 6.3 to help you. For each one, state the reasons why you:

- ◆ might want it on the front page
- ◆ might not want it on the front page.

Paragraph 3 is your conclusion. You should write about the three articles you are recommending. Explain:

- ◆ why you chose them
- ◆ which one you want as your lead story and why
- ◆ why you think this front page will be a success.

2 Write mostly in the present tense.

3 Here are some words and phrases which might be useful:

- ◆ preferable to
- ◆ in comparison with
- ◆ finally
- ◆ however
- ◆ therefore
- ◆ in contrast
- ◆ having considered
- ◆ less/more impact than.

4 When you have finished, read your work to other members of your group. Then use this checklist to help you redraft your writing:

- ◆ Are your points made clearly so that your editor can understand them?
- ◆ Have you mainly used the present tense throughout?
- ◆ Have you set out your ideas in three paragraphs?
- ◆ Is there anything else your editor needs to know?
- ◆ Is there anything your editor does not need to know?
- ◆ Do you need to add punctuation marks?
- ◆ Do you need to correct any spelling?

This unit will help you to:

- develop skills in skim reading
- develop skills in scanning a text
- identify key points in a text
- read between the lines
- draw conclusions carefully.

We read things in different ways, depending on:

- what we are reading
- why we are reading.

Sometimes we need to read carefully and in detail. At other times we may glance quickly over a page to see if it has any relevant information in it. *How* we read is directly linked to *why* we are reading.

Skimming

When you first look at a book you might read the blurb on the back and the introduction. You will probably read these very quickly to get a general idea of what the book is about. This will help you decide whether you want to read more. This type of quick reading is called **skimming**.

Activity 1 ICT

Take one minute to skim the introduction opposite. Decide whether you would use this book to find out more about:

- life on Mars
- alien abduction
- the qualifications needed to be a UFOlogist
- examples of close encounters.

Explain your decisions.

CLOSE ENCOUNTERS

A recent survey in America revealed that 26 per cent of Americans believe that they have seen an Unidentified Flying Object (UFO). That is 90 million people. Thousands of people claim to have been actually abducted by aliens. By this they mean they have been kidnapped and taken on board flying saucers. So can you really be sure it won't happen to you?

If you do come across an alien, it is known as a close encounter. If you just see a UFO it's called a close encounter of the first kind. If the UFO leaves a mark, like a burn on the ground, it is an encounter of the second kind. In an encounter of the third kind, you actually meet an alien. The fourth, and most scary kind, is alien abduction.

Fact or fiction? Thousands of UFO sightings are reported every year. Many are studied by enthusiasts called UFOlogists. They spend their time searching for evidence of Extra Terrestrial life, which means life beyond our planet.

Most sightings turn out to be nothing more than an aircraft, the Moon or weather balloons. But, to this day, over 200,000 sightings remain unexplained, and the witnesses involved remain convinced that they have encountered aliens. Some people think that the kind of person who sees a UFO has an over-active imagination; but can so many people be mistaken?

Case studies This book contains eight case studies. In each study there is an account of a famous close encounter, based on eye witness reports. Each account is followed by an assessment, in which the facts of the story are examined in an attempt to discover what really happened.

Don't panic! It is very hard to prove conclusively whether aliens are visiting our planet. In the end, it is up to you to decide what you believe. If, when you have read this book, you feel that there is strong evidence to suggest that aliens do actually exist – don't panic! If they are here, they have probably been visiting our planet for centuries, and they haven't harmed us yet.

The ability to skim a text is an important skill which improves with practice. In your own reading set yourself time targets and, once you've reached them, try to improve on them. Remember, your aim is to get a general overview of a text.

Scanning a text

Once you have decided you do want to read on, you can use the **index** at the back of the book to find out more about a particular topic. The index tells you what page or pages you need to turn to in order to find the topic you are looking for. Your eyes move quickly over the page until you see the topic you want. This type of reading is called **scanning**.

Here is part of an index taken from a book on UFOs. Try to work out:

◆ in which order entries are placed

◆ how names of people are indexed

◆ how words which have 'the' placed before them, e.g. the Milky Way, are indexed

◆ what to do when an entry has more than one reference.

meteoroid, *see* meteor
Milky Way, 24–25
Moon, 14–15, 23–24
 	
Nazca Plateau, 7
night flier, 11
 	
origins of life, 24
Ozma, 25
 	
parachutes, 22
Perez, Manuel, 1
Phantom jet, 12
photographs, 4, 5
  fakes, 3, 20–21
Pixley, Rex, 1
Project Blue Book,
  10–11, 29
 	
Project Old Blue
	Moon,
	  see Project Blue Book
	pyramids, 6
	
	radar, 12, 25, 31
	radioactive egg, 11
	radio signals, 24–25
	radio telescopes,
	  24–25, 31
	  Green Bank, 25
	reflections, 9, 22
	Report Form, 20
	
	screen UFOs, 18–19
	signal flares, 23
	Socorro, 10
	space creatures, 26–27
	spacecraft, 14
	'Star in the East', 12
	'Star Trek', 18
		stars, 24–29, 31
		starships, 28–29
		
		technology, 6–7, 28–29
		'Trip to the Moon', 18
		
		UFOlogy, 31
		UFOnauts, 1, 10,
		  26–27, 31
		UFOs
		  encounters in space,
		  14–15
		  encounters in the
		  air, 12–13
		  encounters on the
		  ground, 10–12, 28,
		  30
		  landings, 1, 10, 20
		  shapes, 4–5, 9, 11,
		  30
			sightings, 4–5, 8–15,
			  30
			size, 4–5, 11–12, 30
			waves of, 8
			
			Venus, 9, 23
			
			'War of the Worlds',
			  18
			Washington invasion,
			  8
			Westland Wisp, 17
			
			Young, John, 14
			
			Zacatecas, 5
			Zafra, 26
			Zamora, Lonnie, 10

Activity 2 ICT

Using the index, see how quickly you can find the page references for:

a Nazca Plateau   **d** fake photographs   **g** the Moon

b UFO sightings   **e** Manuel Perez   **h** John Young

c radio telescopes   **f** the origins of life   **i** pyramids

When you have found the topic and the page you want, you need to scan it to find the information you want. You know the key words you are looking for and you scan the page until you find them. Only then do you stop and actually read.

Activity 3 (ICT)

Scan the text below to see how quickly you can find the answers to these questions. Take two minutes. The key words have been underlined.

1 What do some experts say the lines on the <u>Nazca Plateau</u> look like?

2 What have the <u>stars</u> got to do with the pyramids?

3 Where have <u>120 ships and planes</u> disappeared?

4 When were the <u>pyramids</u> built?

5 How many ships have disappeared in <u>The Bermuda Triangle</u>?

6 What has helped to <u>spread information</u> about UFOs?

7 What appeared in English fields in <u>1980</u>?

Unsolved puzzles

UFOs are not a new phenomenon. People have been spotting them in the skies for centuries, but until newspapers and television spread information, few people knew about them. According to some researchers, UFOs even visited some of man's earliest civilisations. See what you think.

Help from space?

The pyramids in Egypt were built more than 3,000 years ago, using only very simple tools. They are such an amazing feat of building that some people cannot believe that the Egyptians built them on their own. Did they have help from an alien civilisation with technical knowledge far superior to theirs?

There's no evidence to prove this theory, but the pyramids are the source of many unanswered questions ...

Star power

One mystery surrounds the way the pyramids seem to line up so precisely with some of the stars in the night sky. Can this be just a coincidence, or were the stars especially important to the pyramid builders for some reason?

Dangerous waters

Far more menacing is one theory behind the mysterious disappearance of 120 ships and planes while crossing a triangular area of open sea near the island of Bermuda.

The 'jinxed' area is now known as The Bermuda Triangle. Among possible explanations for the disappearances is that aliens are 'beaming up' ships and planes to join them in space, so that they can find out about life on Earth.

Space signs

The Nazca Plateau in Peru, South America, is the site of another possible UFO puzzle. Broad, long lines and huge animal shapes were cut into rock 1,500 years ago by Indian tribes.

Some experts argue that the lines look like a massive airstrip for UFOs. Did the Indians carve the shapes to show passing aliens what lives on this planet?

Crop circles

In 1980, reports began coming in about circular patches of grain in English fields being mysteriously flattened. As more flat 'crop circles' were found, some argued they were caused by flying saucers landing in the fields.

Scanning helps you to find specific information in a text quickly. Often you are looking for figures or names, as in a train timetable or TV schedule. You will need to develop your scanning skills in all your subjects, particularly when doing research.

Reading for detail

So far, you have looked at the ways you might get an overview of a text (skim) or find out specific information (scan). Often, though, you do need to read a text more closely.

Identifying the key points

The first thing you need to be able to do when reading closely is to follow what is happening. To do this, you need to identify the key points of a text. As you have seen in unit 9 (pages 93–95), each paragraph has its own topic. You can use the paragraphs to help you identify the key points. Read the text on the right about a UFO sighting.

ALIENS IN THE DESERT

Date: July 2nd, 1947
Time: 9:50pm
Place: The Foster Ranch, near Corona, New Mexico, USA
Witness: Multiple witnesses

THE EVENTS

An ear-splitting explosion rang out across the desert. Just thunder, thought sheep rancher Mac Brazel, as he stood on the porch of the Foster Ranch. Yet he still felt uneasy as he watched the stormy night sky.

The next day, Mac rode out to check on his flock. As he paused at the top of a hill to wipe the sweat from his forehead, he suddenly noticed below him something glittering in the sunlight. A trail of wreckage littered the valley floor. It looked like the remains of a plane.

Gossip in town

Three days later, Mac went into the town of Corona for a drink. In the bar, he heard some customers talking about UFOs. Apparently several local people had reported seeing mysterious objects speeding across the sky. Mac wondered whether the strange debris he had found in the desert might be a UFO. He decided to go to the Sheriff's office to report his findings.

So far you have read the small box of factual details and three paragraphs.

The key points from the box are:

◆ 2 July 1947 – 9.50pm – Corona, New Mexico, USA

The key points from each of the paragraphs are:

◆ paragraph 1: Mac Brazel – sheep rancher – heard ear-splitting explosion
◆ paragraph 2: next day found wreckage – remains of a plane?
◆ paragraph 3: 3 days later – Corona – Brazel heard talk about UFOs – reported findings to Sheriff.

Activity 4 WS ICT

Read the rest of the extract below.

1 For each paragraph, make short notes which sum up the key points. Use the examples of paragraphs 1–3 on the opposite page as a model for your notes.

2 Once you have identified the key points of each paragraph, you should have a skeleton outline of the series of events.

Check your outline with that of a friend. Are you missing any key points?

Major Marcel investigates

The Sheriff rang Roswell Airbase, who immediately sent an Intelligence Officer named Major Jesse Marcel to go into the desert with Mac and investigate the wreckage.

What Major Marcel found was unlike anything he had ever seen before. Kneeling on the sand, he examined pieces of the debris. They appeared to be made of some kind of very light metal, like foil. There were little rods with symbols on them. When Jesse tested the debris, he found it couldn't be cut or burned. If he crumpled it up, it returned to its original shape.

Another strange discovery

Meanwhile, 290 km (180 miles) southeast, Grady Barnett stood rigid with terror. While working in the desert, Barnett had come across a strange disk-shaped aircraft that had crashed into a hillside. Strewn around the craft were the bodies of its crew. He moved closer, to get a better look. But what he saw made him freeze with horror.

A strange crew

The four bodies were abnormally thin, with big hairless heads, large eyes and small, slit-like mouths. They were only 1.4 m (4ft 6in) tall. Their arms were long and their hands had only four fingers. They were definitely not human.

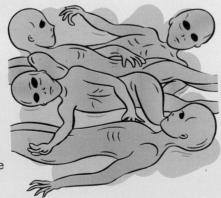

Enter the army

Before Barnett could explore further, a US Army jeep roared up and a troop of soldiers descended on the crash site. They had been alerted by a pilot who had seen the damaged saucer from the air. One officer told Barnett to leave immediately and to tell no one about what he had seen. The soldiers sealed off the area until they had removed every trace of the debris.

That night, transporter planes flew out of Roswell Airbase under heavy guard, taking the crash wreckage to Wright-Patterson Airbase in Ohio.

Alerting the press

At noon the next day, an Information Officer at Roswell Airbase issued a statement which sent local newspapers crazy with excitement: a flying saucer had been found in the desert outside Corona.

Hours later, the airbase issued a new statement. The saucer story was a mistake. The crash debris was only a weather balloon. Reporters were invited to examine the fragments.

Held in isolation

Meanwhile, soldiers were sent to take Mac Brazel into custody. He was held in isolation, safely kept away from press reporters. The only statement he was allowed to make was to confirm the Army's new story.

Nobody knows what threats were made to ensure Mac never talked of what he had seen in the desert. But after his release, he didn't even discuss it with the members of his own family.

Identifying the key points of a text is an important step in understanding it. When making notes on key points you are picking out the essential bits of information only. Your notes should be clear and short.

Implications

Writers often try to influence the way the reader thinks. They may suggest or **imply** certain things without saying them directly. When reading a text closely you need to be aware of what is being implied.

◆ Re-read the opening of the second paragraph:

> What Major Marcel found was unlike anything he had ever seen before

This suggests that there was something very strange about what Major Marcel found, so strange that it was outside his experience altogether.

Now re-read the rest of the paragraph. What details help to reinforce the idea that this metal is very strange?

◆ Sometimes single words can have an impact on meaning. Read this sentence:

> Several local people had reported seeing mysterious objects speeding across the sky.

This tells you that other people had reported seeing strange things. This is not, however, what the writer says in the extract on page 110. She writes:

> Apparently several local people had reported seeing mysterious objects speeding across the sky.

The word 'apparently' is used deliberately to suggest or imply that this may not be a fact. It is a signal to the reader to be careful and think again.

Activity 5

1 Read these sentences carefully. What do they suggest or imply?
   a They were definitely not human.
   b One officer told Barnett to leave immediately and to tell no one about what he had seen.
   c That night, transporter planes flew out of Roswell Airbase under heavy guard, taking the crash wreckage to Wright-Patterson Airbase in Ohio.

2 In the following sentences particular words are underlined. What is suggested by these words?
   a Before Barnett could explore farther, a US Army jeep <u>roared</u> up and a troop of soldiers <u>descended</u> on the crash site.
   b He [Mac Brazel] was held in isolation, <u>safely</u> kept away from press reporters.
   c But after his release, he didn't <u>even</u> discuss it with the members of his own family.

Conclusions

In reading, we draw conclusions. We weigh up the details that have been given to us and use them to help us make a judgement.

Remind yourself of the key points of this text by looking back at your notes. What do *you* think happened in New Mexico on 2 July 1947?

Activity 6 (WS)

Read the statements below. Decide whether you agree (A), disagree (D) or are not sure (?). For each answer give at least *one* clear reason.

1 Mac Brazel found the wreckage of a crashed flying saucer.
2 The metal Major Marcel found was tin.
3 Grady Barnett found the bodies of aliens.
4 Barnett was told not to talk because everyone would want look at the crash site.
5 Roswell Airbase changed their story because they had made a mistake.
6 Mac Brazel was taken into custody because he had made the story up.

Activity 7 (ICT)

The problem with drawing conclusions is that we don't always have the whole picture. Read the next page of the book (below) carefully, then answer these questions:

1 Would you change any of your responses in Activity 6? Why?

2 Imagine you could ask the writer or the people involved in this incident up to *five* questions. What would they be? Arrange them in order of importance.

THE ASSESSMENT

The Roswell Incident, as it is now known, is probably the best known UFO story. Countless wild claims have been made about what really happened.

Project Mogul

In 1994, the Air Force admitted that the balloon fragments shown to reporters at the press conference in 1947 were not the pieces of debris found outside Corona. The fragments the reporters were allowed to examine were from a Rawin Sonde balloon, which was a weather balloon. They claimed that the debris found outside Corona was from a Project Mogul balloon. Project Mogul balloons were designed to carry metal 'listening' discs that were being used to spy on the Soviet Union.

Top-secret tests

It seems probable that what crashed in the desert was a top-secret device that was being tested by the government. Scientists at White Sands missile range, near Roswell, were testing thousands of pieces of military equipment at this time.

Mystery material

Investigators believe that the strange metallic material that had so puzzled Major Marcel when he examined it may have been an early form of polyethylene. Polyethylene had indeed been invented in 1947, and it would have behaved in the manner Marcel described in his tests.

Nuclear weapons

In 1947, the airbase at Roswell was the home base for the world's only airborne combat unit trained to handle and drop nuclear bombs. Therefore, the transport planes seen secretly leaving the airbase under heavy guard on the night of July 8th, were more likely to have contained nuclear weapons than the remains of an alien saucer.

Crash test dummies

On June 24th, 1997, fifty years after the Roswell Incident, the United States Air Force revealed that during the 1940s, experiments were conducted in the area. Crash test dummies were thrown from high altitude research balloons. This might explain the 'aliens' seen in the desert by Grady Barnett.

12 Assignment 3

Read the article on the opposite page. Then answer these questions:

1 Writers use presentational features to organise information and to draw the reader's attention to particular things. List *four* presentational features which help you to recognise this as a newspaper article. **4 marks**

2 Write down:
   a the headline **1 mark**
   b the sub-headings **3 marks**

3 Why do you think the word 'Jaws' is used in the headline? **2 marks**

4 Look at the three pictures in the article.
   a What does each picture show you? **3 marks**
   b Why do you think the writer chose to use colour photographs? Give *two* clear reasons. **4 marks**
   c Look again at the third picture captioned 'Bearing the scars'. Why do you think this picture was used? **3 marks**

5 Copy and complete these sentences:
   Two purposes of this article are to _____ and _____ .
   I think this because _____ . **3 marks**
   One audience of this article is _____ .
   I think this because _____ . **2 marks**

6 In the article the sequence of events is mixed up. Can you work out what happened in the correct order? The first point is:

   Andrew Carter and Bruce Corby were surfing off the coast of South Africa.

   You should make at least *six* points. **6 marks**

7 How does the writer make the reader feel sympathy and admiration for Andrew? Write about:

   ◆ the pictures and the effect they have
   ◆ the things that happened to Andrew
   ◆ the words the writer uses. **9 marks**

8 a What impression is given of the great white shark in this article? **2 marks**
   b Do you think this is fair? Give at least *two* reasons. **2 marks**

9 How would you rate this news article:

   1 – boring   2 – quite interesting   3 – very interesting?

   Write down the number of your choice. Give at least *three* clear reasons, linked to the article, which explain your choice. **6 marks**

TOTAL 50 marks

THE WORLD / TODAY

The man who took on Jaws.. and survived

Lucky to be alive: Andrew Carter with the board he was riding when the great white shark struck in an attack which killed his tragic surfing pal off the coast of South Africa

Andrew back in the swim

BRAVE surfer Andrew Carter displays horrific wounds inflicted by a great white shark.

Beside him rests the bloodied and chewed board he keeps as a reminder of the day he cheated death.

And yesterday, Andrew plucked up courage to venture in the waves again.

It was the first time he had done so since his left leg was almost bitten off by the shark - immortalised in the Jaws films - off South Africa.

Attacked

Doctors had told him that he might never walk again, let alone surf.

Andrew, 32, was determined to prove them wrong.

But he chose less hazardous waters yesterday - at Newquay, Cornwall.

He joked: "I may catch my death of cold here but at least I won't get attacked by a shark. I thought I would never go back in the water again but surfing is my life."

He recalled that he survived the attack because a wave swept him to safety as the 15ft man-eater relaxed his bite to get a better grip.

But then the creature turned and tore at his pal, Bruce Corby, a 22-year-old student, who died a few hours later.

Andrew still gets panicky about the ordeal and has taken nearly a year to recover from his injuries.

Surgeons spent five hours re-constructing his leg with surgery involving hundreds of stitches. Now he has emigrated to England to get over the trauma and works in a Newquay surf shop. Reliving the shark attack, he said: "It had my leg and board in its jaws and was trying to bite through.

"Somehow it loosened its jaws and I slid away.

"I swam for the shore and looked back as the shark was thrashing around and chomping my board.

Victim

"It chased me but couldn't catch me so it went after Bruce and took his leg off

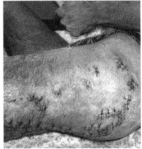

Bearing the scars: Stitches show where surgeons rebuilt Andrew's leg in five hours of surgery

with one bite."

A great white claimed its third victim in two weeks off Hong Kong yesterday.

The creature killed a 45-year-old woman swimmer.

Experts believe the shark could be responsible for other fatal attacks in the area in recent years.

Section D ◆ Writing non-fiction
Introduction

Non-fiction texts are texts which are not poems, stories or plays. They are written for a range of different purposes – to give information, to recount events, to give instructions, to explain, to give advice, to persuade and to put forward a point of view.

In Year 6 you will have written many of these texts: some biography and autobiography, explanations, non-chronological reports and discussion texts. In this section you will extend your learning about how to write non-fiction texts. You will look closely at different types of non-fiction texts to see how they are written before tackling your own writing.

In Unit 13, *Focusing on audience and purpose*, you will learn how to write information texts for different purposes. You will develop your skills in giving clear explanations and instructions.

In Unit 14, *Persuading your readers*, you will learn when and how to adopt a formal tone. You will learn the difference between formal and informal letters and how to write them. You will also learn how to use a range of techniques to persuade your readers.

In Unit 15, *Expressing your point of view*, you will learn about the different styles of writing you can adopt to present your point of view, and also how to use evidence to support your point of view in discursive writing.

Unit 16 tests you on the skills you will develop as you work carefully through the three units.

This unit will help you to:

- match your writing to the needs of your audience and purpose
- identify the features of writing to recount, instruct and explain
- use the features of different types of writing
- use illustrations appropriately when presenting writing.

Purpose and audience

All writers have a reason for writing. This is called the *purpose* of the writing. A text can have more than one purpose.

All writers write for someone. The intended reader is called the *audience*. The audience may be one person, as in a letter to a friend, or many people, as in a letter to a magazine.

When you read a text you can work out the purpose and audience through clues such as:

- what the text is about
- the type of words used
- the way the words and sentences are organised
- the level of difficulty of the words.

Activity 1 ⓦ

1 Work with a partner. Copy and complete this chart by finding clues about purpose and audience in Texts A and B on the next page.

Clues about purpose and audience	Text A	Text B
What is it about		
The types of words used	Simple: e.g. 'push'	More complex and technical: e.g. dandy-horse, principle
Tense used		past
Number of facts in one sentence		Three in sentence 1: 1) 19th century 2) from two-wheeled hobby-horse 3) known as dandy horse/celeripede
Number of words in first two sentences		
How the reader is addressed	'you'	not addressed directly

2 Use the clues you have collected to identify the audience and purpose of each text.

Bicycles

Text A

The first bicycle was a sort of hobby-horse on wheels. It had no pedals so you had to push it forward like a scooter. It was impossible to steer.

You could steer this bicycle by turning the handle-bars. But you still had to push it along with your feet.

This was one of the first bicycles with pedals. Pedalling was very hard work. The pedals went backwards and forwards and drove the back wheel.

Text B

Bicycles developed in the 19th century from a two-wheeled hobby-horse, known as the dandy-horse or celeripede. Around 1840 a Scotsman, Kirkpatrick Macmillan, applied the dandy-horse principle to models with pedals. The first true bicycles, with cranks on their front wheels, went into production in Paris in 1865. Known as velocipedes, or bone-shakers, these wooden-wheeled devices nevertheless popularized cycling.

Activity 2 WS ICT

Use the information below to write a short text for Year 5 children, informing them about the first trains. Your limit is *80 words*. As you are writing for children remember to:

◆ make your sentences short and simple
◆ use short paragraphs
◆ use words that are not too difficult
◆ address the reader directly.

As you are writing about things that happened long ago, use the past tense.

FACTS ABOUT TRAINS

◆ rails invented before trains
◆ horses used on rails
◆ trucks pulled by horses
◆ first railway engines steam
◆ took a long time to build up steam

◆ George Stephenson's Rocket a faster steam engine
◆ could go up to 36 miles per hour
◆ the Rocket built in 1829
◆ the Rocket travelled on new Liverpool and Manchester railway

Recounting events

Many different kinds of writing inform the reader. You have just written a text to inform children about the first trains. Sometimes writers inform readers about things that happened in their own lives, retelling or recounting significant events.

Read the first paragraph of this text and answer the questions that surround it.

My First Bike

How does the first paragraph set the scene?

It was Christmas. Although I had hoped for a bike, I never really expected to get one. When I came downstairs in the morning, there was an enormous parcel under the Christmas tree wrapped in <u>bright red paper with dancing</u>
5 <u>snowmen</u> on it.

What tense is used?

Why is it written in the first person?

As you read on, think about:

◆ the order in which the events are told
◆ the way the writer uses interesting detail to help you picture the event
◆ the words the writer uses to show that time is passing
◆ the way the writer varies sentence length for effect.

For a few seconds I just stared at the parcel in amazement. Then with a sense of great excitement, I pulled off the paper. There it was, a bright blue shiny bike with a gleaming silver bell on the handlebars and a little basket on the front.

That day none of my other presents mattered to me. All I wanted to do was
10 to learn how to ride my bike. After dinner, my dad agreed to give me my first lesson. So, wrapped up warmly against the chilly December wind, I proudly pushed my bike out on to the pavement outside our house. I sat on the seat and my dad patiently held the back of the bike as I tried to keep my balance.

15 It was not easy. He must have got very tired running up and down the pavement supporting the weight of an excited five-year-old, but he never complained.
20 Gradually I learned how to keep the wheels straight and to cycle along without too much wobbling.

25 Finally I could do it! It was like flying!

Activity 3

You probably worked out that the events were retold in the order in which they happened (chronological order). Complete the following questions to check your thinking on the other points.

1 To help you picture the event the writer uses noun phrases. An example of a noun phrase is:

> *bright red **paper** with dancing snowmen*

The noun phrase tells you more about the noun, **paper**. It includes adjectives to describe the noun.

Copy this sentence. Underline the noun phrase in it and say how the detail helps you picture the bike more clearly.

> *There it was, a bright blue shiny bike with a gleaming silver bell.*

2 Just as the noun phrase tells you more about the noun, so adverbs tell you more about the verb. An example of an adverb is:

> *I **proudly** pushed my bike* (most adverbs end in -ly).

Find two more examples of adverbs in lines 11–14. What extra information do they give you about the verb?

3 Some adverbs are used to show time is passing and connect one thing to another:

> ***Gradually** I learned …*

Find one more adverb that the writer has used to show time passing.

4 Some adverbial phrases do the same job as the adverb that shows time is passing, such as:

> ***After dinner**, my Dad agreed to give me my first lesson.*

Find one more adverbial phrase that the writer has used in lines 6–8 to show time is passing.

5 The writer uses sentence length to create a particular effect. Re-read these sentences:

> *I sat on the seat and my dad patiently held the back of the bike as I tried to keep my balance. It was not easy.*

a What is the effect of the short sentence here?

b Try writing two sentences of your own, modelled on these. They could be about learning something new, for example how to swim.

c Find two more examples of short sentences being used for effect. Copy them down and explain:

◆ where they come in the text

◆ why you think the writer has used them.

Activity 4 WS ICT

You are going to recount a significant event in your life. It could be:

◆ when you learned to swim

◆ your first goal

◆ your first day at school

◆ something else.

Follow these stages:

1 Remind yourself of the details of the event by telling a partner about it. Help your partner to picture the event clearly by telling them about it in a lively and interesting way.

2 Start to plan your writing by noting the answers to these questions:

 ◆ Where was it? ◆ When was it? ◆ Who was involved? ◆ What actually happened?

3 Decide how you will set the scene in your opening paragraph.

4 Decide on the order in which you will write what happened. It is usual to follow the chronological order (the order in which things happened).

5 Think about how you will end your writing. A short exclamation (punctuated with an exclamation mark (!)) often works well.

6 Write your first draft, recounting the event. As you are writing about a past event, you should write in the past tense.

7 Read through your first draft. Think about how you could improve your writing by:

 ◆ creating a clearer picture by using noun phrases

 ◆ varying your sentence length for greater effect

 ◆ linking ideas using adverbs and adverbial phrases to show the order of events more clearly.

Adverbs	Adverbial phrases
gradually, suddenly, finally next, later, afterwards, soon	at last, after a while, later on, in course of time

Check your writing for spelling and punctuation. Make sure that your sentences are clear and make sense.

8 Once you have made improvements to your writing, make a final copy.

Writing instructions

You usually find written instructions in recipes, board games and in guides on how to use equipment. Can you think of any other texts that contain instructions? The purpose of instructions is to describe how something is done through a series of logical steps or stages.

Activity 5

Read this text. It is a set of instructions for a children's game called Scaredy Cat. The instructions have not been printed in the right order. In pairs, work out the correct order and start with 1 = A.

A

SCAREDY CAT

B

TO PLAY
Players take a card in turn from the top of the pile.
If it is a Bird card the player places it face upwards
in front of him or her.

C
If it is a Cat card, the player returns the Bird cards, together
with the Cat card, to the pack. The pack is then re-shuffled.

D
How many birds can you collect?
Warning: beware of the Cat!

E
The game ends when the last piece of the Scarecrow is fitted
into place.

F

The winner is the player with the most Birds.
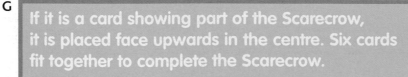

G
If it is a card showing part of the Scarecrow,
it is placed face upwards in the centre. Six cards
fit together to complete the Scarecrow.

H

TO START
Shuffle the cards and place them face downwards.

Check your answers to Activity 5 on page 124. One of the main features of a set of instructions is that they are organised in chronological order – you need to know how to play before you are told when the game ends! Four other important features are:

◆ Instructions often start with a statement or question showing what they are about. Scaredy Cat starts with 'How many birds can you collect?'

◆ Instructions often use imperatives. These are words which tell the reader what to do, for example: '<u>beware</u> of the Cat!'

◆ The points made in instructions are often separated by numbers, letters or bullet points. In Scaredy Cat the instructions are in separate blocks.

◆ Illustrations are often used in instructions. In Scaredy Cat there is a series of icons.

Activity 6

Look at these instructions from another game.

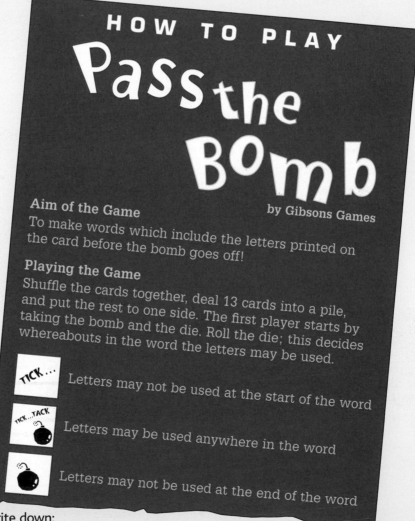

HOW TO PLAY

Pass the Bomb

by Gibsons Games

Aim of the Game
To make words which include the letters printed on the card before the bomb goes off!

Playing the Game
Shuffle the cards together, deal 13 cards into a pile, and put the rest to one side. The first player starts by taking the bomb and the die. Roll the die; this decides whereabouts in the word the letters may be used.

TICK... Letters may not be used at the start of the word

TICK...TACK Letters may be used anywhere in the word

Letters may not be used at the end of the word

Identify and write down:

◆ the statement which shows what the instructions are about

◆ two examples of imperatives

◆ how points are clearly separated

◆ how illustrations help the reader.

Activity 7 ⓦ

Write a set of instructions on how to play either a game such as Snap or a playground game. You are writing for Year 3 children. Follow these stages when drafting your instructions:

◆ Work out exactly what needs to be done and in what order.

◆ Your audience is young. Use short clear sentences to avoid confusion.

◆ Your title should explain what your instructions are about.

◆ Use bullet points, numbers, letters or pictures to separate points.

◆ Use imperatives when telling your reader what to do.

◆ Make it clear when and how the game ends.

When you have completed your instructions, ask a friend to read and comment on how clear and easy they are to follow. Then write your final copy.

Writing directions

Directions are similar to instructions. They tell the reader how to get somewhere. Study these directions. Can you work out the route for this Lake District walk?

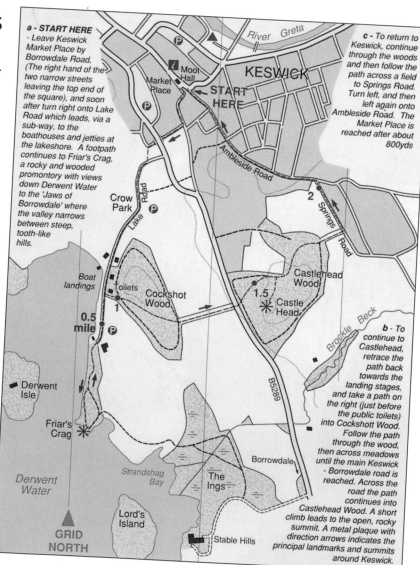

Activity 8

Copy and complete this chart. For each feature listed in column 1, give examples from the map directions in column 2.

Features	Examples
Words which suggest chronological order	soon, after
Imperatives telling the reader what to do	
Alphabet letters to separate points	
Present tense	
Details of what the walker might see	
Illustration	

An illustration can be a very important feature when writing directions. Re-read the directions for the walk. Why and how would the map be helpful to walkers? Would they be able to do the walk if there was no map?

Activity 9

1 Study this map, which shows you part of Blackpool. Draft detailed directions for a walker to get from:

   ◆ Central Pier to Tower World
   ◆ Vance Road to Sea Life.

   Use the features of writing directions listed in your chart in Activity 8.
   When you have completed your directions, ask a friend to check them for you.
   Make changes if necessary.

2 Think of a walk you know well. It could be the walk from your house to:

   ◆ school   ◆ the shops   ◆ your friend's house.

   a Sketch a rough map of the area. It needs to show the main roads and other landmarks such as shops, parks and schools. Label these clearly.

   b Mark the starting point and the finishing point clearly on your map.

   c Write clear directions on how to get from the starting point to the finishing point. Use the features of writing directions from Activity 8 to help you. Remember to include details of what the walker might see.

   d When you have finished, highlight or label the features of writing directions which you have used. Check them against the list in Activity 8. Are there any features you could add to improve your writing?

   e Make a final copy of both your map and your directions.

Writing explanations

An explanation is written to explain *how* and *why* things happen. Read this example of an explanation. Some of the features of writing to explain have been labelled for you.

Text A

Sea water

Sea water contains many minerals, carried there by rivers which flow into the sea. When the sea water evaporates, these minerals remain in the sea and therefore are more concentrated. The most common mineral in sea water is sodium chloride (salt) which makes up about 85% of all the minerals in sea water. As a result, sea water tastes salty.

range of connectives

simple present tense

opening statement to introduce topic

series of logical steps

Now read an alternative explanation to Text A, written in a more lively style.

Text B

Why does sea water taste salty?

A rhetorical question used to involve the reader

When they journey to the sea, rivers travel through many different areas. As they do, they pass over enormous numbers of minerals on the earth's surface. They pick these up and carry them to the sea. The most common of these is sodium chloride – otherwise known as salt!

This makes up about 85% of all minerals in sea water. Gradually the sea water evaporates and the minerals remain in the sea. They are now very concentrated. When you accidentally swallow sea water, you are swallowing enough salt for all the family's fish and chip supper!

River absorbs minerals from land

Main mineral is sodium chloride

River deposits minerals in sea

Sea evaporates

Water tastes salty

Flow chart to highlight main points

Ending that relates the subject to the reader

Did you know?
The Red Sea which borders Africa and Saudi Arabia is so salty that the human body can float unaided.

Extra interesting information

Exclamation for effect

Using a range of sentence structures

In Text B the writer uses a range of sentence structures to make her writing interesting and connect her explanation. She uses:

◆ **Simple sentences.** These contain only one verb:

*This **makes up** about 85% of all minerals in sea water.*

◆ **Compound sentences.** These link two or more simple sentences by using *and*, *but*, *or*. These joining words are a type of connective called conjunctions:

*They pick these up **and** carry them to the sea.*

When simple sentences are joined by a conjunction, each one is called a clause. A clause must have a verb.

◆ **Complex sentences.** These contain a main clause that forms a sentence in its own right, and a subordinate clause that is incomplete on its own:

When they journey to the sea, rivers travel through many different areas.
        Subordinate clause   *Main clause*

The subordinate clause can often be moved within the sentence:

Rivers travel through many different areas when they journey to the sea.
           Main clause   *Subordinate clause*

Subordinate clauses are linked to main clauses by conjunctions such as *when*, *because*, *although*, *as*, *so*, *if*.

Activity 10 ICT

1 Find and copy another example of each of the following in Text B:

> ◆ simple sentence   ◆ compound sentence   ◆ complex sentence.

2 Write your own explanation about how and why things happen.

  a Choose a suitable subject. You may need to do some research. It could be:
    ◆ why we have night and day   ◆ how a _____ works.

  b As you plan your writing remember to:
    ◆ write in the present tense
    ◆ open with a statement or question that introduces the topic
    ◆ follow a series of logical steps
    ◆ end with a sentence that relates the subject to the reader
    ◆ include a flow chart or drawing to highlight the main point
    ◆ use a range of conjunctions, for example *when*, *and*, *because*
    ◆ use a range of sentence structures.

  c When you have written your explanation, ask a friend to read it and comment. Is there anything you can: ◆ make clearer   ◆ make more interesting?

Answers
Activity 5 (p.122) – original order: 1 = A; 2 = D; 3 = H; 4 = B; 5 = C; 6 = G; 7 = E; 8 = F.

This unit will help you to:

- ◆ **choose whether to write in a formal or an informal way**
- ◆ **choose which tense to use**
- ◆ **think about the features of writing to persuade**
- ◆ **select words and punctuation to create particular effects.**

The differences between formal and informal writing

When you are talking to friends you probably speak in a different way from the way you speak to your teachers. You change the way you speak depending on who you are talking to and why you are talking to them. It is the same with writing, including writing to persuade. The way you write depends on your intended audience and purpose.

Read Text A and Text B. Text A is a report for a school magazine about a football match. Text B is taken from a letter in which the same writer tells his friend about the same match. Work through Activity 1 as you read these texts.

Activity 1 (ICT)

1   Which of these accounts uses language: ◆ formally   ◆ informally?
    How can you tell?

2   Full names are given in the report. What nicknames are used to replace these in the letter?

3   In the report you will find the words *football*, *referee* and *brilliant*. What are the shortened, informal forms of these used in the letter?

4   Slang is a term used to describe informal language. An example of this in the letter is: It was absolutely class. Write down any other examples you can find in the letter.

5   What differences in punctuation can you find in the two extracts? Can you give reasons for these? Think about the audience and purpose of each text.

A

Congratulations to the Year Seven Football Team who reached the County Cup Final last week, thanks largely to a late, but brilliant, two-goal salvo from striker Mark Smith. Unfortunately, the game was marred by an ugly incident after the final whistle, involving the opposition team's manager and the referee.

Our boys opened the scoring early on, with James Walker hitting a superb free kick after seven minutes to put his side 1–0 up. By half-time, however, he had been removed from the field for abusive language to an official.

In the second half, play swung from end to end, with a lucky goal from the other team's captain bringing the score to 1–1 – but Smith's two late goals were more than enough to claim a place in the final. We hope that the team can avenge last year's unfortunate defeat, and lift the trophy this time round.

CONGRATULATIONS

B

Talking about footy, you should have seen our school's cup match last week. It was absolutely class – four goals, a red card and a punch-up in the centre circle. The game had everything! We are the best!

You should have seen Jimbo's goal – what a scorcher! It flew right into the top corner – the keeper had no chance. Then he got sent off for swearing at the linesman – but I reckon he was dead unlucky. Anyway, Smithy scored another two in injury time to win it– but their goal was miles offside – it should never have stood in the first place.

Then, right at the end, their PE teacher got really mad with the ref and ended up flooring him! It was brill! I can't wait for the next game, the cup final. With a bit of luck our lads will never be thrashed again. I feel really confident now. We will win that cup!

Thinking about tenses

You will remember that:

◆ the **past tense** is used for writing about events which have already taken place.
For example: Our boys <u>opened</u> the scoring.

◆ The **present tense** is used for writing about things which are happening, or feelings which are felt, here and now. For example: We <u>are</u> the best!

◆ The **future tense** is used to refer to things which are going to happen. For example: our lads <u>will</u> never be thrashed again.

Activity 2

1 Re-read Text A.

   a Find and copy *three* more examples of the use of the past tense.

   b Find an example of the use of the present tense. Write it down. Why is the present tense used?

2 Re-read Text B.

   The writer uses past, present and future tenses. Find and write down *one* example of each. For each example write a sentence which explains why the writer has used that tense. Begin your sentences like this:

   The writer has used the _____ tense here because _____ .

Activity 3

1   Think of a recent school event such as a football match, a music concert or a non-uniform day. Write the first paragraph of a report on this event for the Governors of your school.

Remember to use:

- ◆ mainly the past tense   ◆ full names for people
- ◆ formal vocabulary   ◆ commas to indicate pauses.

2   Write the first paragraph of a letter to a friend about the same event. Remember to use:

- ◆ a friendly tone
- ◆ informal vocabulary
- ◆ the past tense to describe the event
- ◆ the present tense to describe how you feel now
- ◆ the future tense if you refer to future events
- ◆ commas or dashes to indicate pauses, and exclamation marks for effect.

Writing to persuade

If you want to persuade your reader to do something you should:

- ◆ address your reader directly
- ◆ use good reasons to convince the reader
- ◆ use words effectively
- ◆ use short sentences for emphasis.

Look for these features as you read this informal letter, written to persuade:

Birmingham
6th October 2001

Dear Barney,

Thanks for your letter and all your news. Aren't you lucky having days off school? The new neighbours sound good – all of our neighbours are dead boring!

Now for the point of my letter. Can you come to a pizza party and sleep-over at my house at half-term? You'll be able to meet some of my new mates. You needn't be shy about meeting them. They're really nice, honest!

We'll be able to stuff ourselves silly with pizza, watch videos forever and totally chill out. It'll be cool!

My mum says it's OK – she knows how much you love pizza, and she'll get on the phone to your mum to persuade her.

Please say you'll come, Barney. I know you'll have a great time. Be there!

Cheers
Sammy

Activity 4 🌀

1 What reasons does the writer use to persuade her friend? Are they convincing?

2 One way of using words effectively is to exaggerate. Find and copy examples of exaggeration in the letter.

3 Find and copy the two shortest sentences in the letter. What do you notice about the way both these sentences are punctuated? What is the writer trying to emphasise?

4 Why do you think the writer addresses the reader by name at the end of the letter? What persuasive effect might it have?

Activity 5 🔷 🌀

Write an informal letter to a friend persuading them to come on holiday with you. Copy and complete a chart like this to help you gather and organise your ideas:

How I will address my reader:
The reasons I will use:
Words I could use to exaggerate:
Short sentences I could use for emphasis:
Ideas for a short closing sentence:

Remember to:

◆ keep an informal and friendly tone
◆ use informal vocabulary
◆ use tenses correctly when writing in the past, present or future tense
◆ use exclamation marks to emphasise meaning
◆ check your work for spelling and punctuation
◆ make sure that your sentences are clear and make sense for the reader.

Using a formal style

In Activity 5 you used an informal style for your letter to persuade. The next letter to persuade has been written using a formal style. Some of its features have been highlighted for you.

Zop Pops Breakfast Cereals

addresses reader formally —— Dear Sir,

statement of problem —— I am writing to complain about my recent experience with one of your breakfast cereals.

connective to show first stage —— First, I do not expect an unwelcome ingredient in my bowl of Zop Pops. I could hardly believe my eyes when I saw a squashed fly! —— exaggeration for effect

exclamation mark for effect ——

It is fortunate that I had not swallowed it. Can you imagine my distress? —— rhetorical question to involve reader

Such an occurrence is not what I would have expected from the manufacturer of one of Britain's most popular breakfast cereals. Your company has a reputation as a provider of quality foods. That reputation is now in doubt and I am sure you will want to make amends.

personal appeal to reader ——

connective to show next stage —— As a result of this serious matter, I expect considerable compensation that should take into account the shock I received on finding a fly in my breakfast. In addition, I expect to be compensated for my loss of trust in the quality of your products. —— repetition of idea for effect

connective to show last stage —— Finally, you should be aware that I will now have to find another breakfast cereal as nothing would induce me to put a spoonful of Zop Pops near my mouth again.

exaggeration ——

I look forward to receiving your offer of compensation in the near future. —— same idea repeated

formal ending —— Yours faithfully,

James Simpson

J. S. Simpson.

Activity 6

1 What is the writer of this letter hoping to achieve?

2 What reasons are given to persuade the reader that compensation is necessary?

3 Do you think the letter is likely to succeed? Explain your answer.

4 Look at the letter on page 130 and the letter above. What do you think are the *five* most important features of writing to persuade? List them in order of importance.

Read this advertisement carefully. You will be expected to write
a persuasive letter in response to it.

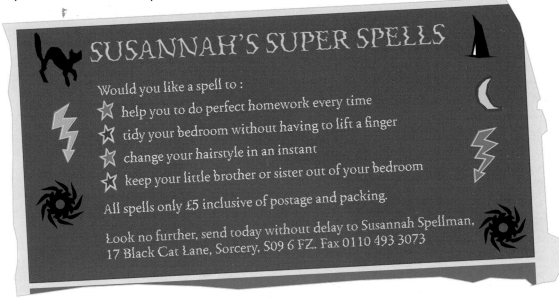

SUSANNAH'S SUPER SPELLS

Would you like a spell to :

☆ help you to do perfect homework every time

☆ tidy your bedroom without having to lift a finger

☆ change your hairstyle in an instant

☆ keep your little brother or sister out of your bedroom

All spells only £5 inclusive of postage and packing.

Look no further, send today without delay to Susannah Spellman,
17 Black Cat Lane, Sorcery, S09 6 FZ. Fax 0110 493 3073

Activity 7 ⓦⓢ

Imagine that it is three weeks since you received your spell and you are not satisfied.
Perhaps your hair has turned bright blue or all your shoes have disappeared.

Write a formal letter to Susannah Spellman, in which you persuade her to return your
money as soon as possible, with additional compensation for the distress caused. Susannah
Spellman may not want to refund your money, so choose your words very carefully to
persuade her.

Use the letter to Zop Pops Breakfast Cereals on the opposite page as a model.
Follow these stages:

1 Plan your ideas under the following headings:

   ◆ how I will begin my letter
   ◆ the reasons I will give to persuade
      Susannah Spellman
   ◆ words I could use to persuade
   ◆ rhetorical questions I could ask
   ◆ how I will use exaggeration
   ◆ ideas I could repeat for effect
   ◆ how I will end my letter.

2 Remember to organise your ideas into paragraphs.

3 When you have written your first draft, read it over
   carefully. If you were Susannah Spellman, would it
   persuade you to refund the money? If not, you need to
   think of some more convincing reasons.

Key words and phrases:

I regret, extremely
dissatisfied,
unfortunate effect,
embarrassed, foolish,
demand, without delay,
I would be grateful,
I cannot recommend

Useful connectives:

first of all, then, in
addition, afterwards, as
a result of this, finally

The language of advertising

Advertisements are persuasive texts. Their writers use a range of techniques to persuade their readers. Read this advertisement headline for Crisis. What does the writer want the reader to feel?

The second person pronoun (you) to address the reader directly

A rhetorical question to make the reader think

Will you give Mary a bed this Christmas?

Now read the rest of the advertisement.

Will you give Mary a bed this Christmas?

Don't leave Mary out in the cold this winter

At 16, Mary ran away from a life of abuse. Today … is homeless. Could … sleep easy on Christmas Eve knowing … was shivering in a bus shelter?

… can help keep Mary, and thousands of vulnerable people like her, safe and warm over Christmas. With £25 from …, Crisis can provide a warm bed, hot meals, clean clothes.

As the days count down to Christmas, nearly 10,000 homeless people are counting on Crisis. …'re counting on … so please send your £25 today – in time to help us buy the bedding, food and clothes. … need to bring Mary in from the cold.

TEMPERATURE AT NIGHT -2°c

Yes, …'ll keep homeless people warm.

Activity 8

1 Look at the picture and read the text of the advertisement. These pronouns have been missed out:

◆ first person singular (I) – 1
◆ first person plural (we) – 2
◆ second person (you) – 4
◆ female third person singular (she) – 2.

Work with a partner to decide which pronoun should fill which gaps.

2 What is the effect of this frequent use of pronouns?

3 The writer refers to one homeless person, Mary, though many are homeless. Why do you think this is done? What effect does it have on the reader?

Using pictures to persuade

Advertisements often contain pictures. These are chosen with great care. Think about the picture in the Crisis advertisement. What does it show you? How is it linked to the writing?

Now look at this picture and think about the questions that surround it.

What is the first thing you notice about these hands?

What words would you use to describe the state these hands are in?

In what ways are the hands different?

Who might these hands belong to?

What might these hands be advertising?

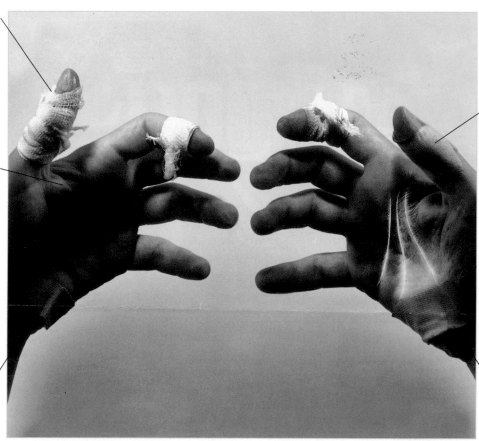

Now read the complete advertisement. Do you think the picture works well?

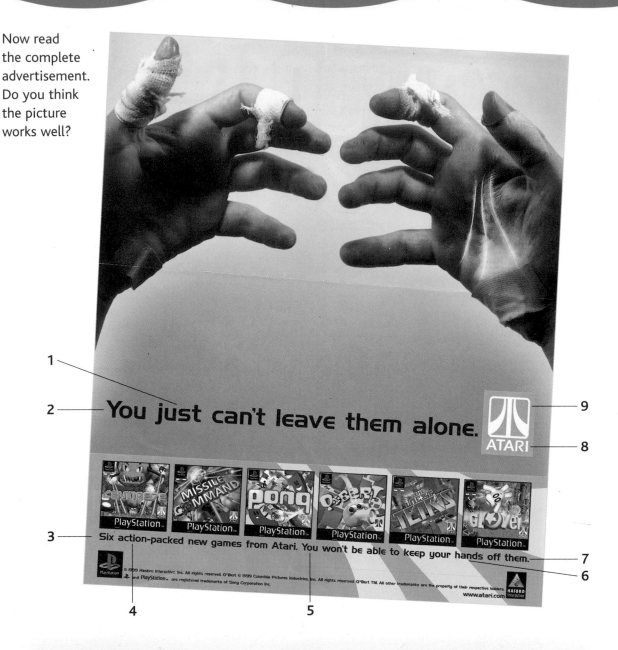

Activity 9

Work with a partner to decide whereabouts on the Atari advertisement these features should be labelled. Match up the features with the numbers on the advertisement. Some features may have more than one number.

a name of maker so buyers can identify product

b readers addressed directly with pronoun 'you'

c easily remembered slogan

d use of informal language

e repetition of idea

f short description of product

g adjectives chosen to make product sound fun

h use of manufacturer's logo.

Activity 10 ICT

1   Draft an advertisement for a computer game or board game of your choice. Your task is to persuade a reader by using a picture and only a few words.
Use the Atari advertisement as a model and these prompts to help you plan your ideas:

   ◆ this is a draft, not a final copy – draw a rough sketch only
   ◆ think carefully about the position of the picture and the words
   ◆ decide how large you will make your picture
   ◆ decide what slogan you will use
   ◆ decide on some adjectives which will make your game sound exciting
   ◆ use no more than 30 words
   ◆ don't forget to use the pronoun 'you' to involve your readers directly.

2   When you have finished your draft, talk to a partner about your work. Can they find the features you have used to make your advertisement persuasive?

Thinking about other persuasive techniques

Writers of advertisements often use a wide range of techniques to persuade their readers. Study the advertisement and also the surrounding notes below carefully. You are going to use these techniques in your own writing.

Puns where writers play with words to amuse the reader and make them think. What does the made-up word 'aquamazing' make you think of?

Imperatives give orders or commands. They are used to persuade the reader directly. Can you find other examples?

Repetition emphasises a particular point. What is being emphasised here?

Superlatives are the strongest forms of adjectives (long, longer, longest). They are used to convince the reader that something is the best of its type. Can you find other examples?

Alliteration is used to amuse the reader and make the words easy to remember.

The use of adjectives makes something sound exciting. Can you find other examples?

Exclamation marks create a tone of excitement and make the reader take note.

Activity 11 🔘

Design and write an advertisement to persuade people to visit your home town or area. Use the persuasive techniques highlighted on the Aquamazing advertisement on the previous page to help you. Follow these stages:

1 Think about how you can make the place sound like somewhere worth visiting. What things about it would you want to draw to a tourist's attention? It could be:

- the scenery
- the shops
- unusual places
- something else.

Remember your aim is to make everything sound better than it is!

2 Copy and complete this chart by making up examples of your own:

Features	Examples	Examples of my own
Use of adjectives to make it sound exciting	Extraordinary – beautiful – welcoming – astonishing	
Superlatives to convince the reader it is the best	The finest example of … The most amazing …	
Puns to amuse the reader and make them think	For the most funtastic time of your life …	
Imperatives to persuade the reader directly	Walk the hills and see … Meet the local people …	
Alliteration to amuse and make words memorable	Cosy cottages Magical markets	
Repetition to emphasise a particular point	Enjoy the best beaches and the best watersports.	
Exclamation marks to make the reader take note	Beware! You'll never want to go home!	

3 Make a rough sketch of the layout of your advertisement, showing the position of:
- the headline
- any pictures you intend to use
- where the writing will go.

4 Draft your advertisement. When you have finished, ask a partner to read and comment on it. Would it persuade them to visit the area you have described? Make improvements to your draft.

Revising what you know about writing to persuade

Throughout this unit you have looked at a wide range of techniques that writers use in order to persuade their readers. Remind yourself of these techniques and make sure you have them written down. You will need them in the next activity and whenever you need to write to persuade.

Activity 12

You are going to design and write a leaflet for the Whale and Dolphin Conservation Society which will persuade Year 7 students to adopt a dolphin. Follow these stages:

1 Study the picture and the information given below.

2 Decide which information you will use and the order in which you will use it. Are there other details you could include?

3 Plan how you will set out your information on the page.

4 Use your knowledge of the features of writing to persuade as you plan your first draft. Any pictures should only be roughly sketched.

5 When you finish your draft, highlight and name all the features of writing to persuade that you have used. If there are not many, you need to include some more.

6 When you are satisfied with your draft, make a final copy. Pictures should be done properly at this stage.

FACT FILE

- Dolphins are threatened by pollution, over-fishing, capture and drowning in drift nets.

- The Whale and Dolphin Conservation Society (WDCS) allows you to adopt a dolphin for the fee of £15.95 per year.

- Dolphin adopters receive a newsletter every six months and an information pack on dolphins.

- Address of WDCS: WDCS Freepost (SN863), SN12 6GZ. Website www.wdcs.org

- Names of dolphins you can adopt: Whisky, a young dolphin often seen in the company of his mother; or two other young dolphins, Sundance and Splash.

- Sundance is a young male, he has an unusual orange spot on his dorsal fin.

- Splash is a young female.

- All these dolphins live in the Moray Firth in Scotland.

This unit will help you to:

- ◆ express a personal view, adding persuasive emphasis to key points
- ◆ think about the features of writing to advise and argue
- ◆ select, sort and organise your ideas
- ◆ write informal advice and consider its effect on the reader
- ◆ validate an argument using evidence to support your point of view.

Writing informal advice

What advice have you been given on occasions when you have asked for some? Think about a time when you have been asked for your advice. Talk with a partner about what advice you gave. A friend or relative may have asked you:

- ◆ how to deal with a difficult situation
- ◆ what to wear to a party.

Usually, when you advise, you give your opinion based on:

- ◆ what you know of the other person
- ◆ your own experience.

It is the same when advice is written. Read this letter and talk with your partner about the advice you would give:

Dear Susie

Please help me, I don't know what to do. Last week I borrowed some earrings from my sister, well, at least, she doesn't know I borrowed them. I wanted them to wear to a party and I knew she wouldn't find out because she was away for the weekend.

But now she will find out, because I lost one of the earrings. I'm really frightened of telling her.

Please could you give me some advice?

Worried of Ilford

Read these replies that agony aunt Susie thought of writing:

A

Dear Worried of Ilford

That was a bad move taking the earrings, wasn't it? I can tell you feel really upset about it now.

How about telling your sister straight away and offering to pay her some money each week until you have paid

for the earrings? That way she won't stay mad at you for long.

Hang on in there. I'm sure it will be OK in the end.

Susie

B

Dear Worried of Ilford

Obviously taking something without permission counts as stealing. You must know this is wrong. You should feel ashamed of yourself.

There is only one honest course of action to take. The right thing to do is to tell your sister straight away what

you have done. You must offer to save up and pay for the earrings as soon as you can.

Remember honesty is always the best policy.

Susie

Activity 1 ⓦⓢ

1   What advice is given in Reply A and Reply B?

2   Copy and complete this table to help you decide which letter would be most useful. Fill in the columns with evidence from the letters.

	Letter A	Letter B
Opening to letter		
Formal vocabulary		
Informal vocabulary		
Sympathetic tone		
Unsympathetic tone		
Use of questions		
Closing to letter		

3   Which reply do you think Susie should send to worried of Ilford? Give *four* reasons for your choice.

Activity 2

1   When you are writing advice it is important that you try to understand the feelings of your reader. It is also important to organise your ideas clearly. Copy and complete this chart to help you understand:

◆ how the ideas have been organised in Reply A
◆ why the writer has used these features.

Feature	Paragraph 1	Paragraph 2	Paragraph 3
Informal language to put reader at ease			
Advice given in the form of a question that involves the reader and makes a suggestion			
Short sentence for impact and reassurance			

Activity 3

Now it's your turn to write informal advice. Read this letter.

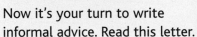

DEAR SUSIE,

I need some help and advice urgently.

Yesterday at school, at the end of the lesson, I saw a good friend of mine put his hand in another student's bag. I couldn't believe it when he took out a CD and put it in his own bag.

I don't want him to think that I'm spying on him or that I'm calling him a thief, but the other student is a friend of mine as well. It isn't fair for her to be treated like this.

I don't want to get my friend into trouble, but I can't let him carry on stealing either.

What do you think I should do?

Anxious

Write the reply you think Susie should make to the letter opposite. Follow these stages:

1 Retell the problem to a partner, to make sure you have understood it properly.

2 Copy and complete this chart to help you organise your ideas.

Stage 1

Words and phrases I could use in the opening of my letter:

Stage 2

My suggestions and ideas for advice are:
How I could phrase it as a question:

Stage 3

My reasons for giving this advice are:

Stage 4

Ideas for reassuring my reader at the end of my letter:

3 Read these reminders before you draft your letter:

   ◆ organise your writing into three paragraphs
   ◆ use questions to involve your reader and as a means of offering advice
   ◆ use some informal language
   ◆ show understanding of your reader's situation
   ◆ use a short sentence for your final message.

Writing advice sheets

Letters to problem pages are written by one person with a problem which is specific to them. Replies to these letters offer advice in an individual and personal way. The advice applies to one person only.

Advice sheets are written for a group of people who all have the same problems or difficulties. They give advice to a wider target audience.

Read the advice below, taken from a leaflet for Year 7 students who are starting secondary school.

Your First Weeks

It has finally come. After spending all summer thinking about it, the first day has arrived and you have started secondary school. You will probably still be feeling _____ and _____ . You might also be a little _____ and _____, but _____ as well. However, there's really no _____ to _____ . Everyone at your new school wants you to _____ _____ .

There are quite a few things which worry new students. The main one is getting lost in your new school, being late for a lesson and feeling embarrassed. If this happens, there is no need to worry about it. You can always ask another student or a teacher where you should go. If you are late for a lesson, you should apologise to your teacher as soon as you get to the classroom. They will understand.

Whatever your worries, you can be sure that everyone will be sympathetic and try to help you with any problems you might have in the first few weeks.

Activity 4

1 Copy out the first paragraph and fill in the gaps with words of your own. Remember that your purpose is to advise and reassure.

2 What is the main purpose of the first paragraph? Find and write down *one* sentence from this paragraph which reassures students. Explain your choice. Why is it important to reassure readers at the **beginning** of the advice sheet?

3 The second paragraph deals with the main worries that students might have. Which sentence explains these worries clearly?

4 Write down the final sentence of the second paragraph. Why do you think the writer chose a short sentence to end the paragraph? If this were a longer sentence, would it have as much impact?

5 Write down one sentence which sums up the meaning of the third paragraph.
Does this paragraph repeat any information from earlier in the text?
Why do you think the writer might want to do this?

Activity 5

The text on the opposite page does not deal with the problems of one person like problem page letters do. It deals with problems that might happen to lots of students. Two of the sentences in the text begin with the word **'if'** to show that these are problems which **might** happen. Copy the sentences out.

1 These sentences are complex sentences made up of:

- ◆ a main clause
- ◆ a subordinate clause.

You will remember that a subordinate clause:

- ◆ is incomplete on its own
- ◆ depends on the main clause to make its meaning clear.

Return to the sentences you have just copied out and underline the main clause of each one. This is the part of the sentence which will make complete sense when written alone.

2 Sometimes the main clause and the subordinate clause are separated by a comma. Explain why you think there is a comma at the end of the clauses starting with 'if' in each of the sentences you copied out.

- ◆ What effect will these commas have on the reader as they read the text?
- ◆ How will they help to emphasise the meaning for the reader?
- ◆ How will they make the reader stop and think?

Activity 6 ICT

1 You are going to write another page for the same leaflet for Year 7 students starting at a new secondary school. Choose one or two subjects that Year 7 students might want advice about such as:

- ◆ homework
- ◆ being late
- ◆ new subjects
- ◆ making friends
- ◆ losing things
- ◆ dinner time.

Use a table like the one below to note down your ideas on what to include. An example has been done for you. Add more ideas of your own.

Subject	Worries	Reassurance	Solution
Homework	Too much	Homework is a worry for most new students	Plan your time carefully

2 Now think about how you will make your advice persuasive and interesting:

- ◆ What title will you use?
- ◆ Will you use formal or informal language?
- ◆ Will you use a serious or a humorous tone?
- ◆ What vocabulary will you include?

Plan your advice sheet in more detail by writing down your ideas under each of these headings:

Paragraph 1

Ideas for reassuring my readers that I understand how they feel:

Vocabulary I could use:

Paragraph 2

My advice for my readers about one particular worry:

Vocabulary I could use:

Paragraph 3

Final reassurance for my readers:

An effective short sentence:

3 Write the first draft of your advice text. Check that you have included the following:

- ◆ good advice
- ◆ some sentences which begin with 'if', to show that you are talking about what might possibly happen
- ◆ comma, if necessary, at the end of the clause starting with 'if'
- ◆ a short sentence to sum up your advice
- ◆ the sort of vocabulary Year 7 readers will understand.

4 Make alterations on your first draft. These may include:

- ◆ crossing out words to replace them with more effective ones
- ◆ taking out words you don't need
- ◆ adding the correct punctuation
- ◆ correcting spellings
- ◆ making sure your sentences are clear and can be understood by the reader.

Now re-read your work to see if it sounds better when read aloud. If you are still not sure, then go back and make some more changes.

5 Make your final copy, including all your alterations.

Writing to argue

Here, the word 'argue' does not mean to pick a quarrel with someone! It means putting forward your point of view. The letter below first appeared in the *Funday Times*, where young people write about topics on which they feel strongly.

Activity 7

Read the letter carefully and answer the questions in the boxes around it.
Your answers will help you to understand how the letter is put together.

Your Views

Dear f-mail,

I'm writing to tell you how manufacturers are ripping off young people. CD singles cost £3.99 but cost only 20p to make. Trainers can cost up to £100 when they actually cost £5 to make. It's a rip-off.

Game console prices are also escalating. First there was Game Boy at £50, next there was PlayStation at £200 and now the Dreamcast sells for £230. When will it all end? Maybe when the PlayStation 2 comes out next year for £300!

Manufacturers – make your profits, but don't take all of our money!

1 Opening statement helps reader understand what the letter will be about.
What is the writer's argument?

2 Sentences in paragraph build up to final short sentence to sum up and repeat the writer's feelings.
What are those feelings?

3 Word which signals first stage in argument.
Which other words signal stages?

4 Rhetorical question (one used for effect).
Why has the writer used this?

5 Punctuation used for effect. Can you find another example?

6 Closing statement to sum up argument.
What is the link between this and the opening statement?

Word bank
escalating – going up fast

Activity 8

1 The writer of the letter on the previous page uses evidence to make their argument seem more reasonable. Make a list of *three* pieces of evidence used to show that manufacturers that they are taking advantage when they charge high prices.

2 Look closely at the first paragraph of the letter.
The first sentence is 'CD singles cost £3.99 *but* cost only 20p to make'. The writer uses the connective **but** to join two contrasting pieces of evidence.

 a Find and write down another sentence in the first paragraph which has the same contrasting technique.

 b Underline the **connective** which joins the two parts of the sentence.

3 Complete the following sentences to provide a contrasting argument. Use one of these connectives or choose one of your own.

> ◆ because ◆ when ◆ as ◆ but ◆ although

 a Teachers believe that students need lots of homework _____.

 b Designer clothes are expensive to buy _____ .

 c Many students think that the school day should finish at dinnertime on Fridays
 _____.

4 The first paragraph in the letter ends with a short sentence for emphasis, to sum up the writer's feelings. Take *one* of the sentences you have just completed. Write a short sentence to sum up and emphasise the point you have made.

Activity 9 (WS) (ICT)

Write your own letter to a newspaper.

1 Make a list of *three or four* things you feel strongly about. Choose one of them to write about ('My argument').

2 Copy this frame. Use it to help you develop your ideas.

My argument		
Four points I want to make		**Evidence I will use**
1		
2		
3		
4		
My ideas for my opening statement		
Words to link my argument		
Rhetorical questions I will use		
Ideas for short sentences to sum up my ideas at the end of paragraphs		
My ideas for my closing statement (don't forget to link this to the beginning of your letter)		

3 Write your letter using the notes you made in the planning frame. Remember to:

◆ organise your ideas into paragraphs

◆ use words such as 'first', 'next' and 'then' to connect your ideas.

◆ use at least one sentence which presents contrasting ideas

◆ use punctuation, such as exclamation marks, to draw attention to your ideas.

4 When you have written your first draft, read it to a partner. Do your arguments convince them? Make improvements before writing your final letter.

Presenting evidence in an impersonal way

Including evidence in an argument can be very persuasive and convincing. It is hard to argue with evidence! Now read the following article taken from a magazine called *Parents Today*. Decide whether the tone is formal or informal as you read.

Computers are Bad for Your Children

PARENTS BEWARE! It has been shown in recent research that computers can be bad for young people. At the recent Parent Child 2000 conference delegates were told by Dr Jane Healy, an American psychologist, that young people who spend long hours at the computer do less well at school.

It has also been revealed by researchers that, by the age of thirteen, young people spend half of their out-of-school working hours in front of either a TV or a computer screen.

Many parents will be shocked by these findings.

Activity 10

1 Compare these sentences from the letter on page 147 and the above article. Which is the most formal? Which words and phrases helped you to decide?

> I'm writing to tell you how manufacturers are ripping off young people.

> At the recent Parent Child 2000 conference delegates were told by Dr Jane Healy, an American psychologist, that young people who spend long hours at the computer do less well at school.

You may have noticed the following about the article:

◆ it doesn't include 'I'

◆ it doesn't use everyday phrases such as 'ripping off'

◆ it uses an impersonal tone: 'delegates were told by Dr Jane Healy that…'; 'many parents will be shocked by these findings'. These phrases use the passive voice. In this article the writer uses the passive voice to put across a convincing and impersonal argument. ⬇

2 Study the table below where parts of the article are written to show the active and passive voices. Explain to a partner:

a what is different about the two sentences

b who the main focus is in each sentence.

Passive voice	Active voice
Delegates were told by Dr Jane Healy that young people who spend a long time at the computer screen do less well at school.	Dr Jane Healy told delegates that young people who spend a long time at the computer screen do less well at school.

3 You may have noticed that:

◆ In the passive voice, 'delegates' stands out and the main action of the sentence is done to them (delegates were told the information).

◆ In the active voice, the name of a particular person stands out (Dr Jane Healy) as it is first in the sentence and she performs the main action (told delegates).

How might it help this writer's argument to take some emphasis away from a named individual?

4 Sometimes it is more persuasive not to name an individual at all: 'it has been shown in recent research...'. Why might this be more convincing than writing, 'I think that computers can be bad for young people?' Where else in the text has the writer used this very impersonal way of presenting the argument?

Activity 11 WS ICT

1 You are going to write a short formal newspaper article for parents arguing that *Computers are good for children*. Gather your evidence. Add to the suggestions below:

◆ recent government research shows that students in primary schools who use computers regularly achieve higher scores in maths, English and science

◆ computers can help with research for homework

◆ computer games can improve children's reflexes.

2 Use what you know about impersonal writing and the passive voice as you write. The following may help you:

◆ it is believed that ...   ◆ it has been revealed that ...
◆ many parents will be surprised ...   ◆ all   ◆ in addition   ◆ furthermore

3 Now write your article. Show it to a partner. Highlight where your writing:

◆ includes factual evidence (more like traditional science writing)

◆ uses formal vocabulary

◆ uses phrases such as 'it has been shown...'

◆ uses an impersonal tone (including the passive voice where individuals are not emphasised in sentences).

You are one of a group of students who have been asked to organise an end-of-year trip to Camelot Theme Park.

Write the following:

1 A letter to your Headteacher persuading them that your year group should be allowed an end-of-year trip.

2 A letter to students containing information and instructions about the trip.

3 A report on the trip after your return, for your Head of Year.

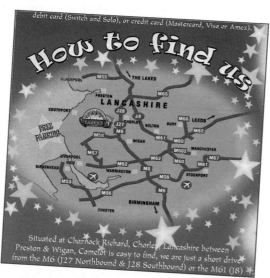

Look closely at the leaflet on Camelot Theme Park shown on this and the previous page.
Make notes on the attractions. Then look at the opposite page for details of each assignment.

KING'S REALM

1 CASTLE ENTERTAINMENT CENTRE
The NEW Jousting Knights dodgems, the amazing Towers of Fun playland and the latest arcade games - all under cover inside our incredible family entertainment centre.

2 NEW
CATS OF THE ROUND TABLE
Don't miss our amazing NEW animatronic show and discover a day in the life of a knight (see back cover for details).

3 CATERPILLAR CAPERS
Perfect for the little ones, this junior rollercoaster is always a favourite.

4 CAMELOT LOG FLUME
It's thrills and spills all the way on this super splashing water ride!

5 VENOM
This terrifying dark rollercoaster ride will have you sssssshaking with fear!

6 PENDRAGON'S PLUNGE
Take the whole family slip-sliding down three breathtaking water chutes - and don't forget the photo!

7 FORMULA-K GO-KARTS
Enjoy lap after lap of high speed thrills on this super karting circuit (extra charge).

Letter to Headteacher

This is a formal letter. Your audience is your Headteacher.

Before you begin to write, make a list of reasons to persuade your Headteacher and number them in order of importance. For example: you have worked hard this year, trips help students and staff to get to know each other, etc.

Plan your letter under the following headings:

◆ opening/closing
◆ a question I will include
◆ connectives to link points: e.g. firstly, another reason
◆ persuasive vocabulary I will use.

Remember to keep your language polite and formal. Aim to write *three* paragraphs.

Key words: deserve, exceptional, behaviour, sincerely

Letter to other students in your year

This is an informal letter. Your audience is students of your own age.

Address students in a friendly and informal way, telling them details of the trip, such as time and date etc.

Give them instructions about the things they need to bring for the trip – packed lunch, snacks for the coach journey, personal stereo, etc.

Explain in more detail what sort of attractions students can expect to enjoy.

Your final paragraph should include a reminder of what fun the trip will be.

Remember to write most of your letter in the *future* tense as you are looking forward to things that *will* happen. Use punctuation such as question and exclamation marks to draw the attention of your audience to your ideas.

Key words and phrases: don't miss it, opportunity, fun-packed

Report for your Head of Year after the trip

Write in clear, formal English. Remember your audience is your Head of Year.

You should write one paragraph on each of the following:

1 the journey to and from Camelot
2 the highlights of the trip
3 details of any accidents and lost property
4 the behaviour of the students on the trip
5 the students' enjoyment of the trip overall.

Remember to write your letter in the *past* tense, as you are writing about events which *have taken* place.

Key words: successful, punctual, rewarding, enjoyable, first aid, lost property office

Section E ◆ Speaking and listening
Introduction

Just as reading and writing are linked, so are speaking and listening. We all talk to ourselves from time to time, but without listeners there isn't much point in speaking! In a sense we are all 'experts' when it comes to speaking – we certainly have a lot of practice every day – but it is very important to develop skills in a wider range of contexts than simple conversation.

In Year 6 you will have taken part in shared discussion, and learned to give a balanced point of view. You will also have used speaking and listening to discuss, evaluate, investigate and explore in a range of situations and for different purposes.

You will be given opportunities to develop your speaking and listening skills in a wide variety of situations in the three units of work in this section.

In Unit 17, *Telling stories*, you will tell a range of stories in different forms, from anecdote to news story. You will learn to structure your talk to suit the situation and the audience.

In Unit 18, *Describing in different ways*, you will learn to make presentations on your own and also work with others in a small group, learning how to work together.

In Unit 19, *Explaining and instructing*, you will learn to use language precisely, in order to explain and instruct, and also how to interview effectively.

Unit 20 tests you on the skills you will develop as you work carefully through the three units.

This unit will help you to:
- ◆ identify some of the differences between speaking and writing
- ◆ structure spoken stories in different ways
- ◆ listen to a variety of speech.

Communicating

You learned to talk before you learned to write. For most everyday communication you speak and listen to people. Most of the speaking is **informal**. If something is **formal** it is probably planned.

Writing tends to be more formal than speaking. Writing is usually organised into sentences and paragraphs, with punctuation to mark out pauses and emphasise meaning. But some writing is 'informal'. Notes, for example, are quite informal. Look at this one:

You've probably left a note like this for someone in your family.

You could say the same thing very formally:

> Mum.   6.00 Thurs.
> At Kev's. Having tea there.
> Back 8.00
>
> Love ya

> 2 Station Road,
> Sadtown,
> Bumbleshire.
>
> Thursday, 1st September
>
> Dear Mother,
>   At time of writing it is six o'clock.
>   I would just like you to know that I am going round to Kevin's house. Kevin's mother has said she will make tea for us. I will be back home at eight o'clock.
>
> With love,

A formal piece of writing, turning the note into a letter, just wouldn't be appropriate. Imagine how your mum would react if you left a note like that!

If you are asked to write an essay or a story, you will end up with something that is formal: it has been planned and shaped. But on the way to writing it you might have:

- ◆ scribbled/jotted down/listed some rough ideas
- ◆ brainstormed ideas using things like spider diagrams.

Those kinds of writing are informal.

You could think about speaking in similar ways. In your lessons you might talk informally about a topic, discuss it in a group or make a presentation.

Activity 1

With a partner, look at the examples below. Work out what you think each situation is.

A

Good morning, everyone. This morning I would like us all to think about what we can do to help the refugees in Kosovo. I am sure you will have seen the pictures on your television screens of the terrible situation the refugees have found themselves in.

B

Hello ... is that Mike? ... Oh, I'm sorry ... Oh ... Do you know when ...? Six? ... Yes, please ... Yes, that would be great ... Bye.

C

It's, well, good. It's like, sort of a lift thing and they strap you in at the bottom – it takes three of you. You go up about ... it's about, I don't know, about 200 feet it must be. Then they stop it at the top and then, wham! you just go rocketing down.

D

Latest reports suggest that up to 60 people have died in what has become one of the worst storms to hit this remote island.

E

A: I'd like to ask you about your previous employment. Could you tell me, please, why you left there?

B: Well, there were two reasons really. I felt I had gone as far as I could in that particular position. I needed a new challenge. And, secondly, ...

F

A: How d'ya get on?

B: Great. Four nil. Murdered 'em.

A: How did thingy ...

B: Becks?

A: Yeah, how did he ...?

B: He played great.

G

Alice: I think it's terrible that people kill foxes. It's cruel.

Bob: Yeah, I agree. All those dogs and people on horses chasing a little animal. It's terrible!

Catherine: I think you are both being incredibly sentimental. Foxes kill other animals in horrible ways – look what they do to chickens.

Dave: Yes, and their numbers have to be kept down. Nobody's suggested how else we should kill them.

Activity 2 WS

Discuss with your partner the different features of the various kinds of talking in Activity 1. Copy and complete the table below.

Informal talk (Nos. B, C, D, E)	Group talk (Nos. E, F, G)	Formal talk (Nos. A, D, E)
Uses slang Incomplete sentences	One person at a time	Uses standard English

Sometimes you have a choice between speaking and writing. If you had an argument with your friend and you weren't talking to each other, you might want to do something about it. You could:

◆ write them a note ◆ telephone them ◆ talk to them face to face.

Activity 3

With a partner, talk through the advantages and disadvantages of each of those methods. What problems might there be in each case? Copy and fill in the chart below, then share with another pair and add any good ideas. Prepare a brief feedback to the rest of the class on each of your findings.

Methods	Advantages	Disadvantages
Write them a note		
Telephone them		
Talk to them face to face		

Narrating

We spend a lot of time telling stories – **narrating** – and listening to them. Stories appear in many different forms in different media:

novels	films	soaps	cartoons	photo-stories
short stories	conversations	television news	newspaper articles	jokes
plays	interviews	dramas	poems	adverts
picture books	songs	photographs	pictures	reports

It may not be obvious that some of these are stories – a photograph, for example. But think about the well known saying: 'A picture is worth a thousand words.'

Activity 4 ICT

Look at the four photographs below. Choose one and make up an interesting story about what lies behind it; tell your story to a partner.

Anecdotes

Anecdotes are short accounts of something that has happened. They are often quite entertaining. We use a lot of anecdotes in everyday conversation. The word originates from the Greek for 'not published', which shows that anecdotes aren't as long or polished as the kinds of stories you find in books. Here is an example:

I can't come out tonight; my mum says I've got to stay in to tidy my bedroom. She went up there on Saturday morning to get my dirty washing and found a plate covered with something she thought was alive! It was the remains of the burgers you and I ate up there two weeks ago! She says I'm grounded till the place is spotless!

That's a little story that's being used to explain something to a friend. It is brief, the characters aren't developed, there is little description and the language is quite straightforward. We use anecdotes like this all the time almost without thinking about it.

Activity 5 ICT

1 **Work with a partner.** Take it in turns to tell three short anecdotes about what has happened to you recently. They could be funny, embarrassing, strange, worrying or unusual things that have happened with friends, with pets, at home or whilst you have been out. Only share stories that you feel comfortable about the class hearing. As you listen to your partner, decide which of their anecdotes is the most interesting and/or entertaining.

2 **Share with the class.** Take it in turns to share one of the anecdotes you have been told. You won't be telling the class your own story, but one that has been told to you. This will test how well you have listened to your partner.

Anecdotes don't really take much shaping. They are usually stories told **chronologically**, that is in the sequence that they happened. The teller usually puts in a few thoughts and comments on the way. They are quite easy to tell because there isn't much background or detail to fill in. Longer stories require more thought and may turn out in a variety of ways.

Telling stories for different audiences and purposes

How you tell a story will depend on who you are telling it to and why you are telling it. For example, you wouldn't expect a news story on television news to begin 'Once upon a time …'

Read the following extract from Ted Hughes' novel, *The Iron Woman*. As you read it, think about how this story is different from an anecdote. It is obviously longer, but can you see any other differences? Make a note of any parts of the story which make it seem particularly *unlike* an anecdote. Share your ideas with others when you have finished reading.

The Iron Woman

About half a mile away a birdwatcher was bent over a bittern's nest, holding a dead bittern and feeling the cold eggs on which the dead bird had been sitting. From his hide, only ten feet away, he had been watching this bird all day, waiting for the eggs to start hatching. He knew the chicks were already overdue. When those first quakes

5 had come, shuddering his camera on its tripod, he had told himself they were distant quarry blastings. He had guessed the strange wailing must be some kind of factory siren. He knew there was a big factory outside the town, only two or three miles away. What else could such things be? And when that second booming wail had come, he had just seen something far more startling. He stared through

10 his binoculars. Two big blowflies were inspecting the eyes of the bittern on the nest. With a shock, he realized the bird was dead. All day, and probably yesterday too, he had been watching a dead bird. This was more important than any noises. So he had waded out, and lifted the dead

15 mother from her eggs. He was horrified. She was quite stiff.

And it was then, as he stood there, thinking that he must take this bird and her eggs to be examined by some scientist, to find out what had killed them, it was then that the third wail came, far louder than the earlier ones.

20 At the same moment the marsh shook, like a vast jelly, and he thought: An earthquake! And maybe that's a siren's warning!

He had made his hide at the edge of some higher ground that stuck out into the marsh from the road.

25 Big bushy willow trees behind him blocked his view of what had terrified the heron and the seagull. But he was alarmed enough by the idea of an earthquake. Cradling the cold eggs in one hand, with the dead bittern tucked under his arm, he collected his camera

30 and returned to his car parked among the willows. As he opened the car door, another jolt shook it.

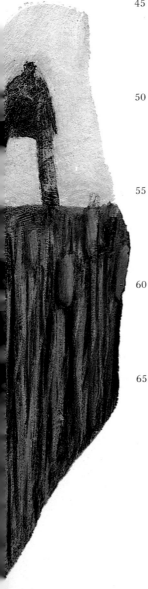

He drove out along grassy ruts on to the road, not far from the bridge where Lucy had stood watching the eel. As he turned right, towards the town, his eyes widened and his brain whirled. The swaying, lumpy, black tower, about a hundred yards
35 ahead, close to the road, could not possibly be anything. Unless it was some structure for aerials, something to do with radar, maybe, draped in camouflage. Even when it moved, he still tried to explain it. Maybe it was a windmill, without arms, being moved – as they move whole houses in America. Or maybe some film company was making a film, a horror film; it could be, and that would account for the hideous
40 noises too. He simply did not know what to think – so he went on driving towards it.

But when it stepped out on to the road directly in front of him, he jammed on his brakes.

This, he could see, was something new. This had come up all on its own out of the marsh mud. Clumps and tangles of reeds still slithered down its black length, with the
45 slime. As it dawned on him what he was looking at, his head seemed to freeze. That was his hair trying to stand on end. Tears of pure fear began to pour down his cheeks. But he was a photographer – and no true photographer ever misses a chance.

He bundled his camera with him out of the car, snatched off the lens cover, and bowed over the viewfinder.
50 Blackness filled it. He backed away, swinging the camera from side to side, trying to squeeze the whole huge shape into the frame. But even before he got it full length he saw, in his viewfinder, that it had picked up his car. Aghast, but also overjoyed, he took shot after shot as the great figure slammed his car down on to the road, raised it high and slammed it down again, and again, and again, like somebody trying to beat
55 the dust out of a heavy rug. The birdwatcher remembered, with a fleeting pang, the bittern's eggs. They had been nested in his cap on the passenger seat. But he forgot them as he saw the paint and glass exploding, like steam, each time the car banged down on to the road. Doors flew off, wheels bounded into the reeds, and the mouth in the head opened. As the terrible siren wail came out of that mouth, the
60 birdwatcher turned and ran.

Fast as he ran, he wasn't fast enough. The black, mad giant bounced the twisted, steel-bright tin can of a car into the reeds, then gouged up a handful of marsh mud clotted with weedy roots.

The birdwatcher thought the swamp monster must have caught up with him and
65 kicked him. But it was the flung mass of mud that slammed him from behind, wrapped round him and swept him many yards along the road. He struggled out of it and clutching his greasy camera, spitting out the foul black mire, and sodden, he ran for his life.

*from **The Iron Woman** by Ted Hughes*

Word bank
mire – soft mud or dirt

Activity 6

You are going to retell the story by Ted Hughes in a different way. This activity will help you get the events of the story clear in your mind.

Working with a partner, prepare a list of the things that happen to the birdwatcher in the extract. Begin with the first thing that happens and work your way through the main events chronologically, that is in the order they occur. Copy and complete a chart like the one below:

What happens	How the birdwatcher feels
He watches the bittern on its nest	He's a little surprised that the eggs haven't hatched
He hears some strange 'wailing' and feels the marsh shaking	He's not particularly worried about the sounds and the quakes
He goes to the bittern's nest	

The story is in written form. You are now going to approach it as a spoken story.

Activity 7

In your pairs, decide which of you is going to be the birdwatcher. The other will be a police officer.

Imagine that after the events of the story, the birdwatcher rushes to the police station in a panic. A police officer asks him to calm down and say what happened. Remember that the story will seem very far-fetched to someone who was not there. Will the birdwatcher be believed?

Whichever of you is going to be the birdwatcher should look again at the events of the story and the kinds of emotions the birdwatcher went through. Use the chart from Activity 6 to help you. Don't attempt to tell the whole story, just try to capture the panic that you, as the birdwatcher, felt. Tell your story and then the police officer will want to ask you some questions.

The police officer's role is:

a to listen carefully to the story without interrupting

b to ask questions which a sensible person who has heard a fantastic story might want to ask.

When you are ready to begin the role-play, close this book so that the written story isn't in front of you. Use your written notes if you need to.

When a story appears in the media – in the newspapers, on television or radio – it has to be changed. One reason for this is that the way the story is told must be right for the audience. Another reason is that it can only be given a limited amount of space, so unimportant things have to be left out and the main points emphasised.

Activity 8 WS ICT

Work in pairs. Imagine that the birdwatcher's story reaches local radio. The person in charge of radio news wants to include it, but can only devote 30 seconds to it.

1 What angle will you take? Here are some ideas:

Serious story

◆ The birdwatcher's film has been developed and shows disturbing photographs of what looks like a metal monster.

◆ The police are unable to explain what happened to the birdwatcher's car.

◆ The birdwatcher has a theory linking the pollution which seems to have killed the bittern to the iron woman.

Light-hearted, entertaining story

◆ An ordinary accident damaged the car and put the birdwatcher into a state of shock so he made the whole thing up.

◆ The film in his camera was damaged.

◆ No one else has seen this 'metal monster' so it is likely to be imaginary.

2 Think about how you are going to shape the story for the news bulletin. Copy and complete this chart.

What happened?	
When did it happen?	
Where did it happen?	
Who was involved?	
Why did it happen?	

◆ Together decide which of the answers are most important in this story. Decide on the order in which you are going to tell the story.

◆ Remember the focus is the *speaking* aspect of what you do, so work out how it is to be told, the tone of voice, any emphasis and so on.

◆ Before you start, work out how long your news story can be. Choose a page at random in this book and read it aloud. Stop after 30 seconds. Count the number of words spoken. That is how many words you can use.

3 Write out your script and read out your story to the rest of the class.

4 Discuss with your partner what you have learned about how to structure spoken reports.

Drama

Drama is an important means of telling a story. Work in groups of three or four on the activity below.

Activity 9 (ws)

Awkward situations can lead to good drama.

1 Choose *one* of the following situations as the basis of a scene you are going to write for a short radio play.

a A young person has been accused of shoplifting. The shop manager has called the police. The police officer, manager and young person are in the manager's office. The young person's mum or dad has been telephoned and is just about to appear.

b The parents of two children have been divorced for about a year. The mum or dad has met a new boy/girlfriend and brings him/her home for the first time so that he or she can meet the children.

2 Before you begin to write your scene, decide together on the following:

◆ what issues you want to act out

◆ how you can make your characters interesting and different from each other

◆ how your scene will begin and end

◆ any dramatic techniques that would make your play interesting, for example 'freeze' action, a character speaking directly to the audience or the use of silence to create tension.

After you have talked through the points above, **improvise** in a small group. This means you act a scene out in a rough way without a script, seeing what happens.

3 Write the script of your scene. Remember:

◆ to show differences between characters by the way they speak and their mannerisms (such as saying, 'like' or 'you know' a lot)

◆ to use stage directions that advise on how the words should be spoken

◆ to include any sound effects

◆ the audience cannot *see* what is going on.

If you have access to a computer, use it to write out your scene.

Dramascript is set out in ways that make it easy to follow: use **bold** for the characters' names and *italics* for stage directions. It makes it easier to read. If you don't have access to a computer, think of ways of showing these things.

This unit will help you to:

◆ **describe things clearly**

◆ **consider different ways of describing things**

◆ **speak in a variety of situations.**

Describing people clearly

Activity 1

Work in groups of three or four. Take it in turns to tell each other about someone who is important in your life, choosing someone you feel comfortable about describing to others. Give the group a flavour of the person and why they mean a lot to you. Your important person could be:

◆ a relative – your mum or dad, perhaps

◆ a friend – one you have now or from when you were younger

◆ a famous person you admire

◆ a person from history

◆ a character from a book.

The others in your group may ask you questions to help draw out information and to understand your feelings.

Activity 2 ICT

Following on from Activity 1, you are now going to make a presentation on your own. Describe to the class the person that you chose in Activity 1. Your talk should last a maximum of *two minutes*. Following Activity 1 you should have a few ideas about what to say and what you might want to change from your first thoughts.

You will need to decide on the following:

◆ what kind of approach will make my talk interesting

◆ what am I prepared to share with my audience and what do I wish to remain private?

Planning

1 Your talk must have a shape. In Activity 1 you were sharing ideas with other students in an informal way. Your presentation will be more formal, more organised. Shape your presentation by breaking it down into sections. Organise your thoughts by filling in a chart like the one below.

Physical description: what they look like/wear	
Description of mannerisms/personality/behaviour	
Why they are important to you	
Anecdotes that bring your person to life	

2 Think about whether you'll begin by telling your audience who the person is, or whether you want to create suspense by not telling them until the very end. It could come as a surprise to find out that the person they thought was your mum is actually a character from a cartoon! Putting a 'twist' like this into a talk shows that you have planned and shaped it. It also makes it more interesting.

3 Think about the following:

◆ If you are going to talk to a quite large group of people, try to have eye contact with as many individuals as possible in the group. It helps them relate to you.

◆ The use of gestures – a shrug of the shoulders, raising the eyebrows, spreading your arms, tapping a finger on a desk for emphasis – can help add impact and make your talk more lively.

◆ Try to avoid reading a script word for word. It is better to have an outline and use some prompt cards – something to glance down at. Below is an example of some prompt cards used by one student who was talking about her baby brother:

1.
He's lovely looking:
chubby
hair
bright clothes

2.
Personality:
Noisy
Happy when ...
Miserable when ...

3.
Some of the things he gets up to:
The dog anecdote
The wedding anecdote

4.
Why I love him:
He needs looking after
END: He's my baby brother and he's very important to me.

Describing things effectively

In America, many years ago, a young director was producing a radio version of a book called *The War of the Worlds*, a story about a Martian invasion of Earth. To make his radio drama interesting and believable the director began the drama as though it were a news flash interrupting a dance-music programme. Thousands of Americans, hearing the 'news' and thinking it was true, panicked and fled from their homes. This incident shows the power of radio and the power of words.

The War of the Worlds

PHILLIPS: Ladies and gentlemen, this is Carl Phillips again, at the Wilmuth Farm, Grovers Mill, New Jersey. Professor Pierson and myself made the eleven miles from Princeton in ten minutes. Well, I … I hardly know where to begin, to paint for you a word picture of the strange scene before my eyes, like something out of a modern *Arabian Nights*. Well, I
5 just got here. I haven't had a chance to look around yet. I guess that's it. Yes, I guess that's the … thing, directly in front of me, half buried in a vast pit. Must have struck with terrific force. The ground is covered with splinters of a tree it must have struck on its way down. What I can see of the … object itself doesn't look very much like a meteor, at least not the meteors I've seen. It looks more like a huge cylinder. It has a diameter of …
10 what would you say, Professor Pierson?

PIERSON: *(off-mike)* What's that?

PHILLIPS: What would you say … what is the diameter?

PIERSON: About thirty yards.

PHILLIPS: About thirty yards …

Following further interviews with Pierson, and having gone back to the studio for more music, this dramatic commentary was heard:

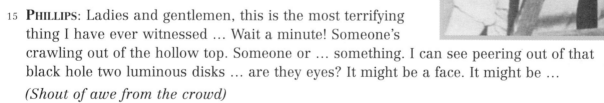

15 **PHILLIPS**: Ladies and gentlemen, this is the most terrifying thing I have ever witnessed … Wait a minute! Someone's crawling out of the hollow top. Someone or … something. I can see peering out of that black hole two luminous disks … are they eyes? It might be a face. It might be …

(Shout of awe from the crowd)

20 **PHILLIPS**: Good heavens, something's wriggling out of the shadow like a grey snake. Now it's another one, and another. They look like tentacles to me. There, I can see the thing's body. It's large, large as a bear and it glistens like wet leather. But that face, it … Ladies and gentlemen, it's indescribable. I can hardly force myself to keep looking at it. The eyes are black and gleam like a serpent. The mouth is V-shaped with saliva
25 dripping from its rimless lips that seem to quiver and pulsate. The monster or whatever it is can hardly move. It seems weighed down by … possibly gravity or something. The thing's rising up. The crowd falls back now. They've seen plenty. This is the most extraordinary experience. I can't find words … I'll pull this microphone with me as I talk. I'll have to stop the description until I can take a new position.
30 Hold on, will you please, I'll be right back in a minute.

Activity 3

With a partner, read the conversation between Phillips and Pierson aloud; try to capture the right tone for Phillips especially. Then discuss the following:

1 What tricks have been played on the listening audience to make them think this is real, rather than a drama?

2 What is the effect of Phillips using the present tense as he describes what he sees?

3 How does Phillips use language to make his eye-witness account dramatic?

Activity 4

Prepare a short radio talk (up to one minute) on one of the following imaginary scenarios:

◆ You are an astronaut. You have landed on Mars. You radio back what you can see.

◆ You are a space explorer. You have landed on a new planet. A strange creature is approaching you. You broadcast back what you can see.

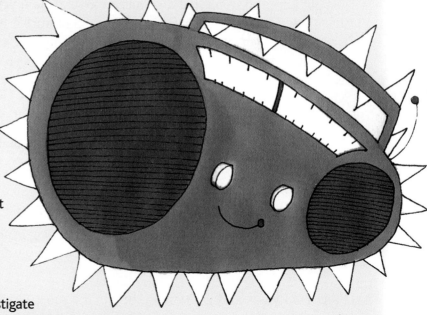

◆ You are a radio reporter. You have heard stories about UFOs locally and you have gone to investigate. You set up your recording equipment and then a UFO appears. Describe what you see.

◆ You are a radio reporter. You have been asked by your boss to go and investigate a 'haunted house' story. You don't really believe in ghosts, but just as the clock strikes twelve you see something ...

◆ You are a radio reporter. There have been sightings of a strange beast in the local woods. Your boss asks you to go and investigate. You start to describe the wood and what you can see when suddenly something moves in the undergrowth ...

Remember that when you are trying to describe things that others cannot see, you have to find the words to make things clear. Here, you are at the scene and things are happening before your very eyes. You will be talking in the *present tense*.

Working in groups

Working in a group isn't as formal as, for example, making a presentation, but it isn't the same as an informal chat amongst friends either. In Activity 5 on the next page, you will be asked to work in a group in quite a structured way.

The small uninhabited island of Mortonia has recently been visited by you and your group. This is an artist's impression of Mortonia.

You are going to make a five-minute radio programme in which you describe the island. The purpose is to entertain by sharing your thoughts on the unspoilt beauty of the island with your audience. You want to give an impression of a lovely landscape which should not be harmed by tourism or other development. Remember that your listeners will have to imagine the beautiful island you are describing.

Activity 5 ICT

Work in groups of three or four. Appoint a chairperson to lead the discussion, keep everyone involved and check the time.

The group will also need to appoint a scribe to jot down decisions.

The following activities should be directed by the chairperson:

1   Spend a few minutes discussing the advantages and disadvantages of having to do this on radio. What are you going to have to do to make your description interesting?

2   Spend some time looking at the map of the island. Discuss the different aspects you could describe. Use your imagination to fill in details. The chairperson must make sure everyone is involved. As group members come up with ideas there may need to be decisions taken. Everyone should have responsibility for a part of the programme. Here are some suggestions:

    ◆ each person could be given a particular part of the island to describe
    ◆ each person could choose a different aspect of the island such as wildlife, the river, the coast or the island at night.

3   Once you have sorted out a structure, think about the details of parts of the programme. Think of what you can see, and also other things you can describe:

    | ◆ sounds | ◆ smells | ◆ touch | ◆ feelings | ◆ thoughts. |

4   Decide on a style. Will you imagine you are there on the island, with a tape recorder, speaking about your immediate impressions of the island? Or do you want to imagine you are back home again and that your programme is based on notes and memories?

    If you choose the first way, you might find whoever is speaking saying things in the present tense:

    This must be the most beautiful place on earth. I'm standing on a deserted, golden beach with the warm water lapping at my feet. Behind me are …

    Whereas the second way might be in the past tense:

    I spent a lot of time by the sea. The beach was a thin strip of golden sand. In the mornings when the tide went out I'd often find …

5   Tape your programme if you can. You could perhaps include sound effects.

6   When you have finished, discuss how effectively you worked together as a group:

    ◆ If you did the same thing again would you change your group approach?
    ◆ Did you keep to the task efficiently?
    ◆ Did it help to have a chairperson?
    ◆ Was each group member given a full role?

This unit will help you to:

◆ **use language precisely in different situations**
◆ **listen carefully**
◆ **use language that is suitable for your audience.**

Explanations

If you explain something you are making it clearer and easier to understand. An explanation gives reasons as to *how* or *why* something happens. Explanations need to be organised in a sensible way that helps others understand them.

Activity 1

Work in groups of three or four. Your group is to be a panel that is in charge of awarding prizes, like the Oscars, for the best in a particular category. The occasion is quite formal.

a Choose *one* category from the following:

◆ soaps
◆ magazines or comics
◆ novels
◆ computer games
◆ singers
◆ living heroes and heroines.

b Produce a list of possible contenders for the award – no more than four.

c Discuss the good and bad points of each.

d Decide on a winner; you must have clear reasons for your choice.

e When you have finished, work together to produce a speech in which you will explain the judges' decision.

Use appropriate language. It is not enough just to describe your favourite: you must **explain** your decision.

Use the following frame to help you choose appropriate language:

A greeting:

'Ladies and gentlemen …'; or 'Girls and boys …'

'The list of entries for this year's best [fill in the category] award was …'

'The winner this year is …'

'I would now like to explain the panel's decision. There were X reasons …'

'First' or 'Most importantly' '… it was felt that …'

'Secondly…' and perhaps 'Thirdly, …' or 'Another strong point in its favour …'

An ending:

'Finally …' or 'Therefore …' or 'In conclusion …'

Instructions

Instructions tell you *how to do* something. Instructions have to be very clear so that they can be followed easily. Children's TV presenters often give instructions to their viewers on how to make things.

Activity 2 ICT

Work in pairs. There are two origami diagrams: A (a boat) below and B (a house) on the next page. One of you should choose A and the other B.

Make your chosen origami model so that you know how to do it. You may have to do it several times. Once you are confident about making it, unfold it again. Now you're ready to give instructions on how to do it.

1   Whoever chose Diagram A will begin. Your task is to explain to your partner how to make the origami model boat, following the numbered stages in the diagram. Your partner will have a piece of paper and will only do exactly what you tell them. You must be very clear in what you say. It is very important that the listener only does exactly as they are told – not what they think they should do.

2   When you have finished you should discuss what was helpful and what was not.

3   Then swap, so that the person who chose Diagram B can explain to the first person what to do to create an origami house.

4   Again, talk about what was helpful and what was not.

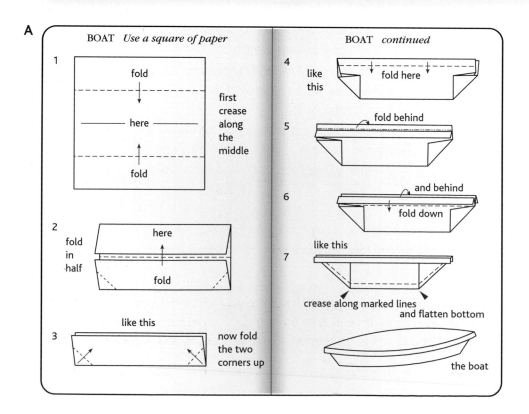

B

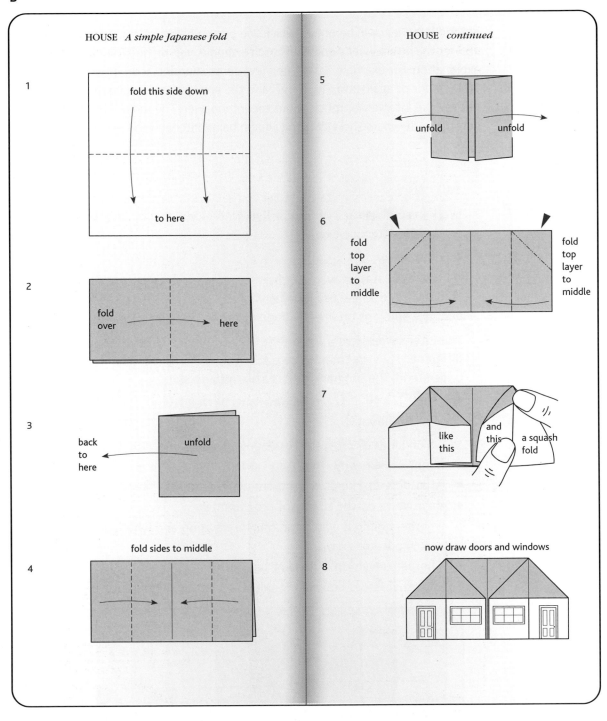

HOUSE *A simple Japanese fold*

1 fold this side down

to here

2 fold over → here

3 back to here ← unfold

4 fold sides to middle

HOUSE *continued*

5 ← unfold   unfold →

6 fold top layer to middle   fold top layer to middle

7 like this   and this   a squash fold

8 now draw doors and windows

5 When you have both had a chance to give and receive instructions, discuss what you have learned about how to give clear spoken instructions. Write down a list of bullet points which offer good advice on how to give instructions well.

Interviews

A good interview will be one in which the person being interviewed, or interviewee, doesn't just answer the interviewer's questions with a simple 'yes' or 'no'. They will follow it with some explanation. For example, in an interview on fox-hunting, if an interviewer asked the question, 'Are you for or against fox-hunting?' and the answer was 'for', it would be a very dull answer and not tell the interviewer much about the interviewee. The more interesting answer would be 'For, because ...' It would show that the person being interviewed has a thought-out point of view.

Activity 3 ICT

Work in small groups of four or five. One of you will be an interviewer and the others will be the interviewees.

The interview

A local radio station wants to feature more local young people. A decision has been taken to have a new programme which will allow listeners to hear various young people's opinions on a wide range of topics.

The interviewer is very important because they will be responsible for drawing out the different views and making sure that the opinions are clear enough for an audience to understand. The programme has a six-minute slot.

The topic for the first programme is to be 'Television'. The programme-makers would like to hear about:

◆ which kinds of programmes young people enjoy/dislike and why; interviewees might explain why they like a particular programme or kind of programme
◆ what different kinds of programmes they would like to watch
◆ their views on the timing of programmes
◆ whether children watch too much television and whether it is turning them into 'couch potatoes'
◆ whether television is good or bad for young people
◆ any other issues concerning television which seem important.

Pre-production

◆ Before the programme is produced, the group need to discuss some of the issues so that the interviewer can find out what different interviewees have to say. The interviewer also has to think about the order in which they ask people to talk. This discussion will not be as formal as the final programme. However, it is not a group 'chat'.

◆ The interviewer should lead the group and ask each group member questions. Interviewees should be able to put forward constructive arguments in support of their viewpoints. They should also be able to discuss each other's views. One member might listen to someone's point of view and then say something like: 'That's a good idea; you could add on ...'; or 'Wouldn't it be better to say it like this ...'

◆ It is the interviewer who controls the group. As well as managing the discussion, the interviewer should be listening out for particularly interesting points of view that are well expressed. He should 'push' people to explain what they think. Group members should help each other to express views clearly and fully. Here are some of the ways in which each member could contribute to this discussion and help move the group forward:

> 1 Listen for things you agree with; perhaps you might be able add more detail and further arguments.
>
> 2 Listen for things you disagree with; perhaps you might be able to provide a different opinion: 'I disagree because...'
>
> 3 There may be some areas of discussion that you know quite a lot about. You might be able to say: 'Did you know that ...' and provide an anecdote or some facts that might help make something clearer.
>
> 4 Leave it to the interviewer to lead the discussion, but if you feel the group is 'stuck' you might make a suggestion to them: 'Wouldn't it be a good idea to talk about ...?'

◆ Following this discussion the group, led by the interviewer, decides on the shape of the programme: in what order they will approach the different issues and what kinds of questions will be asked. There should be no 'surprises' in the programme.

Production

After rehearsal, the interviewer writes their introduction and ending to the programme.

The script should be fairly simple:

◆ introduction – a greeting followed by a brief outline of the topic under discussion, before the people being interviewed are introduced

◆ ending – a summing up of the main issues, a thank you to the panel and a goodbye.

The programme will be performed in front of a live audience.

Plan a presentation to the class on the subject of 'Love and Hate'.

Your talk should be divided into two equal parts. One half will be about things you love and the other half about things you hate. In total it is to take no longer than *three minutes*.

The talk is an opportunity for you to describe the things you love and hate, to explain why you feel that way and to narrate anecdotes to help bring your talk to life.

Preparation

Begin by thinking about and making a list of things you love and hate. Try to have some variety in your list – some serious things and some light-hearted ones.

Once you have decided on a list, start thinking about how much to say about each thing. You probably won't be able to use all of them – there isn't time. There might be one in particular that you know will take up quite a lot of time. Perhaps you'll have quite strong feelings about a couple of things and decide to talk about those in detail.

On the other hand, you might prefer to include a lot of things and just mention each one briefly.

It's up to you.

Audience and purpose

Your audience is the class and your teacher. The purpose is to give a talk that will interest and/or entertain them. You might decide that some humour would be a good idea. Everyone in your class will be giving a similar talk, so it's important to try to be a little bit 'different'.

Getting ready

You will probably need some prompt cards. Don't write out a complete script – it's meant to be a talk, not a reading.

You could begin: 'I'll tell you what I love …' or 'I'll tell you what I hate …'

What makes a good talk?

Your audience would say that if they are interested – that is, if you are interesting – then it's a good talk.

> A good talk:
> ◆ is organised – it doesn't ramble
> ◆ has some variety of tone
> ◆ is clear and easy to listen to.

Section F ◆ Words: spelling strategies and vocabulary
Introduction

The following units will help you to:

◆ learn and remember spelling strategies
◆ understand the link between handwriting and spelling
◆ apply spelling rules
◆ use a dictionary and thesaurus effectively.

First find out what sort of speller you are by answering the questions below.

How well do you spell?

Look back over some pieces of your own writing, and make a chart like the one below. On a scale of 1 to 5, tick the appropriate box to show how far you agree (1) or disagree (5) with these statements:

a I spell more words correctly than incorrectly in my own writing.

b When I misspell a word, it's usually only one or two letters that I get wrong.

c In each sentence that I write, I never spell more than two words incorrectly.

d I know how to use a dictionary to check spellings.

e I can read lots of words even if I don't know how to spell them all.

	1 (agree)	2	3	4	5 (disagree)
a					
b					
c					
d					
e					

If you got mainly 1s, congratulations!
You're on the way to being a good speller. Read on and you'll find lots of useful tips to help you improve even further.

If you got mainly 3s, you're starting to gain confidence with your spelling. Read on and by the end of the year, you'll be joining the 1s.

If you got mainly 5s, then you probably think you're worse at spelling than you really are! The good news is that a lot of people feel the same way as you do and that you can do something about it. Read on ...

This unit will help you to learn spelling strategies and keep a record of your progress.

Spelling mistakes are usually made for very small and simple reasons:

- a letter has been missed out of the word: watch ✓ wach ✗
- an extra letter that is not needed has been added: watch ✓ whatch ✗
- some letters have been written the wrong way round: watch ✓ wathc ✗
- a letter that makes the same sound has been used instead: watch ✓ wotch ✗

Activity 1 Spotting patterns to improve your spelling

Look back through your own writing. Have you made mistakes like the ones above? If so, note down those words. Circle the parts of the words that you got wrong, and note down their correct spelling. Use the strategies in this unit to practise getting them right.

Activity 2 Using spelling strategies

Even though writers of all ages spell most words correctly most of the time, few people think of themselves as good spellers. People often feel that making three or four mistakes in one piece of writing is bad spelling. They forget that they got all the other words right. To be a confident speller, first be positive about what you can already do.

- Some people learn how to spell words by creating a picture of the word in their heads:

  sep**A**rate

- Some people find it helpful to sound out the word into its separate syllables:

  par + tic + u + lar + ly

- Others need to write out the word to find out if it feels right:

  necessary ✓

Most people use a combination of these ways. Choose *three* words that you often misspell. Using the above strategies, practise getting them right.

Activity 3 Look, cover, say, write, check

Another well-known strategy for learning a word is the sequence *Look, Cover, Say, Write, Check*.

> A **Look** at the word first for a few seconds.
> B **Cover** the word or shut your eyes and see if you can 'see' it in your head.
> C **Say** the word by slowly breaking it up and pronouncing each bit separately, e.g. *diff+er+ent*
> D **Write** the word from memory. Try to see it in your head as you write.
> E **Check** the word to see if you are right. If not, look carefully at the part of the word that you find difficult. Then start the sequence again.

Choose *three* words that you often misspell. Use the above strategy to practise getting them right.

Activity 4 Tracking your progress

Keeping a record of your spelling progress will help you to get better at spelling. Here are some useful strategies.

1 **My words to learn**: make a note of errors from your work and set yourself targets:

> although – target: to remember –ough
>
> beautiful – target: to remember –eaut
>
> caught – target: to remember –aught

2 **Mnemonics**: remember spellings by using rhymes and pictures:

beautiful =	**b**	**e**	**a**	**u**	tiful
	bendy	**e**lbows	**a**re	**u**seful	

3 **Plurals**: record the rules that often catch writers out:

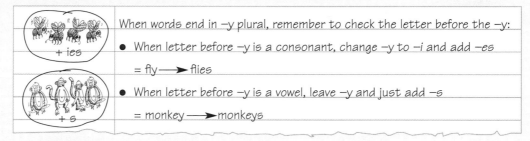

When words end in –y plural, remember to check the letter before the –y:

● When letter before –y is a consonant, change –y to –i and add –es

= fly ⟶ flies

● When letter before –y is a vowel, leave –y and just add –s

= monkey ⟶ monkeys

4 **Key spelling rules**: note down spelling rules that are helpful to you.

5 **Spelling investigations**: keep notes of investigation results, such as:

- ◆ **brainstorms** of words that follow particular rules and conventions
- ◆ **diagrams** of word roots and families
- ◆ **columns** of words organised according to letter patterns.

6 **Dictionary**: build a mini-dictionary of everyday words that you find tricky, for example:
- ◆ actually ◆ although ◆ beautiful ◆ because ◆ caught ◆ health

7 **Words linked to different languages**: note down words that are linked to other languages:

> petit/petite ⟶ small in French
>
> petite ⟶ small in English

8 **Key words from other subjects**: make a note of words that have a meaning that is special to a subject and/or different from everyday use:

Science	Maths	PE	D & T
absorb	addition	activity	aesthetic
acid	angle	agility	brief (means 'instructions' not 'short')
alkaline	amount	athletic	carbohydrate
amphibian	approximately	biceps	component

Using a dictionary and thesaurus

Activity 5 Using a dictionary with speed and skill

Using a dictionary to find a correct spelling is another useful strategy. Did you know that a dictionary can be split into four parts called 'quartiles'?

a   Take a dictionary and try the following:

> ◆ open it around the middle: you will find that it usually falls open at the letter **M**
> ◆ open it again half-way between A and M: it usually falls open at the letter **E**
> ◆ open it again half-way between M and Z: it usually falls open at the letter **S**

When you are looking for a word, think of the quartiles of the dictionary: **A–D; E–L; M–R; S–Z**, and go quickly to the right section. This mnemonic (memory trick) will help you remember them more easily:

> All B C D
> Elephants F G H I J K L
> Make N O P Q R
> Squirts T U V W X Y Z

b   Use the quartiles. Race your partner to find the meanings of the following words:

1 affluent	**2** yacht	**3** serious	**4** declare	**5** bereft
6 stride	**7** gloat	**8** timid	**9** cautious	**10** incentive

c   Once you have the right quartile, how do you quickly find the word you are looking for? First find the letter the word starts with. The words are then listed in alphabetical order by the rest of the letters in the word:

2nd letter	3rd letter	4th letter	5th letter
sang	slant	strange	straddle
sent	sleep	stretch	straggle
sing	slip	string	strap
song	slop	strong	straw
sung	slurp	strung	stray

Write down these words in the order you would find them in a dictionary:

fade	fire	feather	flint	fiddle	fin	first	feeling	fury	fling

Activity 6 Using a thesaurus to improve your writing ◀ICT▶

A thesaurus helps you to find a variety of words with the same or similar meaning. It can help you build a wide vocabulary and make your writing more interesting.

Use a thesaurus to look up *five* words that you know are overused by many writers.

You could start with alternative adjectives for *big, nice, beautiful, scary* and *bad*. You could also look for verbs that could replace *walk, say, move, laugh* and *run*.

Note down alternatives that you could use instead.

Spelling and handwriting

Researchers have found a clear link between spelling and handwriting. Students often need to write a word to find out if it 'feels right'. This is known as 'muscle memory'. Those who learn to write in a consistent form of joined-up handwriting have a better chance of learning letter patterns this way.

There are two basic movements involved in fluent handwriting:

◆ the arm moves the hand across the page
◆ the fingers make the shape of the letters.

Activity 7 Building your 'muscle memory'

1 Make sure your writing arm is supported (put your weight on the opposite hand or arm). Holding your pen, move your arm and hand across the page without moving your fingers.

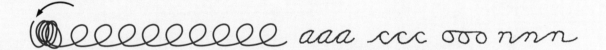

2 Now move your fingers while keeping your hand and arm still. As soon as you know the correct way to form your letters, your handwriting practice should focus on writing words or common letter combinations e.g. *ight, ough, ness, tion, ous, ted*. This will help you build them into your 'muscle memory'.

Handwriting tips

◆ Don't try to change your writing completely. Instead, identify one or two things in your own handwriting that you're not happy with and focus on these.

◆ Experiment with different ways of holding the pen or positioning the paper. Make sure you hold the paper with your non-writing hand.

◆ Don't give up on joined-up handwriting because you can't join two or three problem letters. Keep trying! Remember, getting used to joining patterns of letters will improve your 'muscle memory' for spelling.

◆ Frequent short practice sessions will have most impact on your handwriting. Aim to spend 5–10 minutes at a time on practising your handwriting.

◆ Write with a fountain pen or a fibre-tipped one rather than a ballpoint.

ICT This unit will help you to learn how letters make different sounds in different words.

Activity 1 Hard and soft letter sounds

p.9

Look back at the story of Persephone on page 9. Copy this chart showing words the writer uses that contain the letter *c*.

Paragraph 1	Paragraph 2	Paragraph 3	Paragraph 4	Paragraph 5
protected	forced	concerned	conference	cold
crops	place	because	discuss	comes

1 Read the words aloud and listen to the way the letter *c* is pronounced.
   a What sound does the *c* make when it's followed by a consonant such as *t*?
   b What sound does the *c* make when it is followed by the vowels *a* or *e* or *i* or *o* or *u*?
   c What sound does *c* make when it's followed by the letter *y*, as in *cycle*?

2 Find more words that contain the letter *c* in the story of Persephone. Add them to your chart. Circle words where the *c* sounds hard, as in 'cold'. Tick the words where the *c* sounds soft, as in 'forced'.

> **Remember:** *c* is usually soft sounding when followed by *e, i* or *y*.

Activity 2 Letter combinations making the same sound

p.9

You will improve your spelling by knowing that different letter combinations can make the same sound. The following words are from the story of Persephone:

◆ yielded	◆ trees	◆ plead	◆ secretly

1 Read the words aloud. What vowel sound do they all share?

2 There are four ways of spelling the same vowel sound in these words. Write them down.

3 Make a chart with four columns – one for each spelling of the sound. Now look through the story of Persephone. Find more examples of words with this vowel sound. List them in the right column.

Activity 3 Unstressed vowel sounds

p.10

1 Vowel sounds can be difficult to hear in some words, and writers often misspell them. Read the following words aloud.

◆ different	◆ conference	◆ generally	◆ generous	◆ modern
◆ interesting	◆ miserable	◆ desperate	◆ pattern	◆ reference

2 Explain to a partner which part of the word is often not pronounced when spoken aloud.

3 Say all the words aloud in an exaggerated way so that the part that may be misspelled is heard more clearly. Break each word into separate syllables: diff + er + ent and write them down. Now turn to 'Beowulf' on page 10. Write down words with tricky vowel sounds. Practise using this strategy to make sure you spell them correctly.

This unit will help you to work out the rules for making singular words into plurals.

Activity 1 Different ways of making words plural

1 Read the poem 'U.S. Flies in Hamburgers' on page 28. Some of the plural words are listed below.

p.28

Plural	Singular	Plural	Singular	Plural	Singular
fries	fry	beetles	beetle	leeches	leech
flies	fly	roaches	roach	peaches	peach
pies	pie	onions	onion	days	day

2 Look closely at the endings of the plural words. In order to be made plural, what happens to a singular word that:

◆ ends in -y with a consonant before the -y (e.g. fly)?

◆ ends in -y with a vowel before the -y (e.g. day)?

◆ ends in -ch (e.g. peach)?

> Write down the rules for turning each of these types of words into plurals.

Activity 2 When to add –es

1 Read this list of plural words aloud. What do you notice about how –es plural words sound? Think about the number of syllables in these words.

◆ bushes	◆ toys	◆ buses	◆ meals	◆ babies	◆ dishes
◆ trays	◆ cities	◆ parties	◆ days	◆ churches	◆ foxes

2 Turn the words in the box above into singular words and write them down. To do this, choose from the following options:

a take off –s   b take off –es   c take off –ies and replace with –y

Activity 3 Words that end in –f

Singular words that end in –f or fe follow two main spelling patterns for making them plural.

1 Write down the singular spellings of the words below. Use a dictionary if you need help.

◆ calves	◆ selves	◆ halves	◆ reefs	◆ knives
◆ sheriffs	◆ cuffs	◆ wives	◆ roofs	◆ lives

2 You will notice that two spelling rules apply to these singular words that end in –f or fe. What are they? Sort the words into two columns based on the spelling rules they follow. What spelling rule applies to words ending in –ff?

24 Breaking words into syllables

 This unit will help you to work out how words are built, and so spell them correctly.

A **syllable** is a unit of sound. Breaking words into syllables and sounding them aloud is a good way to help you spell a word correctly. Using this strategy with a word such as *diff + er + ent* means that you spell the *er*, and don't write '*diffrent*'.

Look at the way the following words have been broken up into syllables:

2 syllables		3 syllables		4 syllables	
picture	pic+ture	carefully	care+ful+ly	photographic	pho+to+graph+ic
number	num+ber	regular	reg+u+lar	impossible	im+poss+i+ble
kitchen	kit+chen	estimate	es+ti+mate	introduction	in+tro+duc+tion

Activity 1 Sounding out syllables

p.31

1 The words below, from the poem 'Muddy Boots' on page 31 have two, three or four syllables. Read them aloud, break them up into syllables and write down the words showing the syllable breaks. There is at least one tricky word!

- ◆ trudging
- ◆ country
- ◆ splodgely
- ◆ thlodgely
- ◆ criketty
- ◆ slimy
- ◆ horrible
- ◆ fallomph
- ◆ gallooph

2 Write down other words from the same poem that have two, three, four or more syllables and show where you think the syllable breaks go.

> **Apply the strategy:** sound out the syllables with a partner. Take it in turns to spell the words. See how close you can get to the poet's spelling just from sounding the word out very clearly.

Activity 2 Research syllables for yourself

1 Make your own collections of *two-*, *three-* and *four-*syllable words. For each word you choose, show the syllable breaks. Can you think of any words with *five or more* syllables? Group them in columns according to the number of syllables.

2 Choose one word from each group, or from each column in the table at the top of the page, that you may not always spell correctly. Using the strategy, practise getting them right.

> **Remember** Dividing words into syllables in order to sound the word out clearly will help you spell words with tricky vowels and letter patterns.

ICT This unit will help you to learn about word families so you can understand unfamiliar words and spell more accurately.

pp.33

In the description from *The Sword in the Stone* on page 33 lines 1–5, Merlyn is described as wearing a flowing gown covered in *signs* of the zodiac. This word is often misspelled without the *g* but it is easy to spell if you remember it as part of a family of words. Sign is a word root because other words are made from it. These are known as **derivations**.

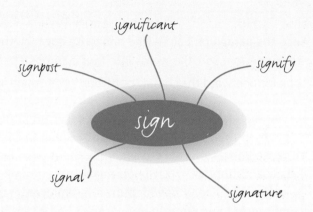

Activity 1 Looking for the family link

With a partner, try to think of as many words as you can to go into the word families of the word roots in the box below. Use a dictionary to help you. Write up your findings for each word using a diagram like the one above.

| ◆ act | ◆ child | ◆ take | ◆ bore | ◆ light |

Activity 2 Taking family investigations further

pp.33–34

Now write diagrams for other words you can find that belong to word families in the extract about Merlyn on pages 33–34. Use a dictionary to help you. For example:

The old gentleman was a singular <u>spectacle</u>. ◄——— word root *spect* from two Latin words meaning 'to look at', 'to watch'.

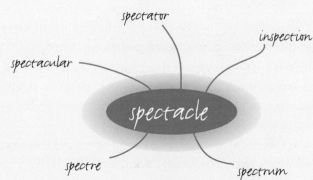

26 Word endings that sound the same

 This unit will help you to spell correctly word endings that sound the same.

Sometimes it can be difficult to know how to spell word endings when there are two or three possible ways of spelling the same sound. The word endings *-cian*, *-tion*, *-ssion* and *–sion* are used for a large number of words but they can sound exactly the same, for example *description*, *permission*. Words ending with a *–zion* sound are usually spelled with *–sion*, as in *vision*. How do you decide which spelling to use if you are unsure?

Activity 1 Which is the most common ending?

p.33

1 Read the paragraph below. Find and write down all the words that end in *–cian*, *-tion*, *-ssion* or *-sion*. Sort the words into four columns. The first three are underlined.

2 Look for one word that has a *-cian/-tion/-sion* sound in the *middle* rather than at the end.

> You might have already read the <u>description</u> of the <u>magician</u>, Merlyn, on page 33. Magicians are thought by some to cast spells, make <u>explosions</u> and cause confusion: they often act without permission! You might have seen presentations of wizards on television, in films or have read about them in books. Magicians have featured in children's stories throughout the years with great variation in appearance and character. Some have been described in a traditional way like Merlyn in the passage on page 33. Others are more up-to-date creations without a cloak or a wizard's hat. Whatever their form, the conclusion must be that wizards in stories have certainly held the imagination of many people.

3 Now add to your columns with words that you use every day. Try to think of at least six *–tion* words, four *–sion* words, one *–ssion* word and one *–cian* word. Check the spellings in a dictionary if you're not sure.

4 Which ending is the most common? Which ending is the least common?

Activity 2 Finding clues and searching for patterns

From the previous activities you will have seen that the most common type of ending is *–tion*. For more clues about which ending to use when you're not sure, you will need to look closely at the words you have collected.

Find examples in your columns of words that follow these patterns:

- *-tion* words that often follow a long vowel sound, e.g. ov*a*tion, completion, promotion, poll*u*tion
- *-sion* words that sound like *-zion*, e.g. vision
- *-cian* words that are often made from words that already ended in *c* and are often linked to jobs, e.g. physi*cian* and politi*cian*.

> Record the patterns you have discovered. Remember them to help you spell word endings correctly.

This unit will help you to recognise whether a word is an adjective, noun or verb by its letter pattern and also help you to spell it correctly.

Words can be **modified**, or changed slightly, to make them into adjectives, nouns or verbs. Letter patterns often tell us what job a word is doing in a sentence.

Activity 1 Ways of recognising adjectives

pp.39–40

1   Look at the description of the Grand High Witch on pages 39–40. Some of the adjectives that describe her end in the suffixes *–ful*, *-ing*, *-ed*, *-some*. These are common to many adjectives. Find and list as many adjectives with a suffix from the passage as you can. Underline each suffix.

2   The jobs that words do can be changed by adding, removing or changing their endings. Copy out the example below which takes the words *worrying* and *frightful* and shows you how the modified (changed) words work in a sentence. Complete the chart.

adjective (describes a noun)	noun (an object or feeling)	verb (often indicates action)
1 The witch's face was worrying.	Her face was a worry to me.	Her face worried me.
2 The witch's face was frightful.	I had a …	Her face …

Activity 2 Word-match investigations

To make an adjective or a noun into a **verb**, the suffix is often removed or changes to *-en*, *-ify*.

To make an adjective or verb into a **noun**, the suffix is often removed or changes to *-tion*, *-ity*, *-ness*.

1   Copy and complete the following chart. Match the adjective to its noun and verb from the choices in the box below. Underline the suffix. The first one has been done for you.

Adjective	Noun	Verb
clear water	clarity/clarification	clarify
solid ice		
related matters		
dark night		
simple problem		
connected thoughts		

- ◆ solidify, solidity
- ◆ relation, relate
- ◆ darken, darkness
- ◆ simplicity, simplify
- ◆ connect, connection

Remember Changing, adding or removing a suffix can change a word into an adjective, noun or verb. List the main suffixes you have learned about and indicate what kind of word they often make.

28 Common confusions

This unit will help you with words that sound the same but are spelled differently, and tricky letter patterns.

Words that sound the same but have different spellings and meanings such as *too, to, two* are called **homophones**. You need to be extra careful that you have used the right word and spelling if you are writing using ICT and a computer spellchecker. A computer spellchecker will only tell you if you *misspell* a word. You could spell a word correctly but use the wrong word for the sentence. For example:

> I am not <u>aloud</u> out tonight

'aloud' would not be picked up by a computer spellchecker

> *aloud* meaning 'out loud' should be *allowed* meaning 'have permission'.

Activity 1 Checking for homophones

Check the following sentences for incorrect homophones and write out the sentences correctly. The first three words that need replacing are underlined. One sentence has two homophones!

p.24

> 1 Because she lost the game of squash, she ~~through~~ *threw* her racquet on the floor.
> 2 <u>Their</u> are many reasons for learning to spell.
> 3 Holding his audience spellbound, he spoke <u>allowed</u> with confidence and expression.
> 4 Before going skiing, it's advisable to check the whether reports.
> 5 Righting is easier now that I'm better at spelling witch means I don't worry so much!
> 6 If you listen carefully, you will be able to here what they are saying.

Read Benjamin Zephaniah's poem on page 24. Which homophones have been used incorrectly on purpose?

Activity 2 Grouping words by letter patterns

Some words are difficult to spell because their written letter patterns don't seem to match their sound. An example of this is *light*. Some of the letters are silent. A good way of learning words with tricky letter patterns is to remember them in groups.

p.43

1 Find three words with silent letters in lines 8–12 of the story *Rice without Rain* on page 43. Make a table like this one, and write them in the correct column.

–aight	–ight	–eight

2 Now use your own knowledge to add to each group. If you are unsure about how to spell some of your words, check them in a dictionary first.

3 Make a similar table for words with the letter patterns: -ough -ought -aught. Start with: cough, thought, caught.

This unit will help you to use apostrophes for omission and possession.

◆ **omission** – one or more letters have been missed out e.g: 'isn't' *the o has been missed out*

◆ **possession** – something belongs to something else, e.g: 'the dog's tail' *the tail belongs to the dog*

Activity 1 Investigating how apostrophes are used

p.58

Read the script from *How Green Are You?* on page 58. Under two headings, 'Omission' and 'Possession', list examples of words that use apostrophes.

Activity 2 The apostrophe of omission in the right place

Writers contract words in informal writing, making the words shorter. Copy and complete the chart by writing the words in full so they sound more formal. The first word has been done for you.

When you contract a word in your own writing, always remember to put the apostrophe in the right place.

do not	don't
	I'm
they are	they're
	we'll
	we've
	it's
	isn't
	you're

apostrophe goes where letters are missed out

Activity 3 Apostrophes to show possession

The following sentences all contain words with apostrophes of possession.

◆ The wolf's teeth are very sharp. (*the teeth belonging to the wolf*)

this is only one wolf so simply add apostrophe +s

◆ The wolves' teeth are very sharp. (*the teeth belonging to the wolves*)

'wolves' already ends in s, so there is no need to add another s, just add an apostrophe

1   Use the examples above to help you rewrite the paragraph below. You will need to add *six* apostrophes of possession in the correct places. Watch out for plural words that do not need an apostrophe at all.

> Alisons brother, Peter, has just been made striker for the local football team, Camberley Challengers. He plays on Sundays and practises each week. His teams well-loved mascot is a huge hedgehog called Harry! This year, the teams efforts have been amazing but the Challengers changing rooms are badly in need of repairs. The showers leak and the footballers clothes often get wet. They hope Alisons fund-raising ideas will solve the problem.

2   Warning! The following possessive pronouns do not have apostrophes:

◆ his	◆ hers	◆ ours	◆ yours	◆ theirs

There is no apostrophe in 'its' when it does not mean it is:

◆ *its* means 'of it', as in 'the team had its mascot'.

◆ it's means 'it is' as in 'it's a huge hedgehog!'

This unit will help you to get to know the different types of word endings so you can work out the meaning of unknown words and improve your spelling.

Activity 1 the suffixes -ed, -ing

p.64

1   Look at the columns of verbs below. How are the words in column A different from the words in column B? Why do similar words have different endings?

A	B	A	B
climbed	climbing	interrupted	interrupting
decided	deciding	reacted	reacting
explained	explaining	surprised	surprising
faced	facing	tasted	tasting

Did you realise that column A shows the verbs in the *past* tense and column B shows how the ending changes to make the verb *continuous*?

2   Take away the suffixes *–ed* and *–ing* from the words above. Write down the words that are not complete. What do you need to add to make them into full words?

3   Work out the rule for what you need to do with a word that ends in 'e' when you add *–ed* and *–ing*. Write it down.

4   Now check to see if this spelling rule has been used for the verbs included by the writer in *Tuck Everlasting* on page 64.

Activity 2 the suffix –ful

1   Check that you recognise all the adjectives ending with the suffix *–ful* in the box below. Use a dictionary to look up any unfamiliar words.

◆ beautiful	◆ careful	◆ delightful
◆ frightful	◆ merciful	◆ peaceful

2   Now take away the suffix *–ful* from the words above. Write down the words that are incomplete.

◆ What letter would you need to change in order to make them complete?

◆ Which words are already complete? Can you see why?

3   How many more *–ful* words can you find and investigate? You could use a dictionary, other texts and your own writing as sources.

Remember

◆ When adding the suffix *–ed* and *–ing* you usually, if the word ends in e, drop the e before adding the suffix: care ⟶ car~~e~~ ⟶ caring

◆ When adding *-ful* (a suffix beginning with a consonant) to words that end in e, there is usually no need to drop the e: care + ful ⟶ careful

◆ When adding *-ful* to words that end in y, if the letter before is not a vowel, change the y to an i then add *-ful*: beaut~~y~~ ⟶ beauti ⟶ beautiful

31 What are prefixes?

 This unit will help you to spell unfamiliar words by identifying prefixes.

- A suffix is a group of letters added to the end of a word to change its meaning: play ⟶ play**ful**.
- A prefix works in the same way but it is added to the *front* of the base word: play ⟶ **re**play.

By knowing about prefixes, you will be better able to spell words you have not seen before by breaking them into familiar parts.

Activity 1 Are there spelling rules for prefixes?

When adding prefixes to words, you usually just add the prefix without changing the spelling of the base word: **un**cooked, **over**cooked, **under**cooked. If the last letter of the prefix is the same as the first letter of the base word, you just double up the letter. For example,

> dis (*prefix*) + satisfied (*base word*) = dissatisfied
> un (*prefix*) + necessary (*base word*) = unnecessary

Mix the following base words and prefixes to make complete words. Write them down. Some base words can take more than one prefix. If you're not sure whether you have created a real word, use a dictionary to check.

Prefix		Base word	
◆ dis	◆ over	◆ appoint	◆ necessary
◆ in	◆ im	◆ possible	◆ regular
◆ ir	◆ under	◆ stated	◆ believable
◆ mis	◆ un	◆ conduct	◆ credible
◆ re		◆ reversible	◆ spent

Activity 2 Researching prefixes

Extend what you know by researching how prefixes make different words. Copy the chart below. Use a dictionary to find at least *three* complete words for each prefix. The first two words using the prefix *anti* have been done for you.

Prefix	Complete words		
anti	1 anticlockwise	2 antifreeze	3
dis			
in			
mis			
ir			
over			
pre			
re			
under			
un			

32 Reviewing your spelling progress

This unit will help you to revise what you have learned about spelling.

Take time to stop and reflect on what you have learned. Answer the following questions:

- What do you know now that you didn't know before?
- What words have you learned to spell?

Activity 1 Reviewing personal spelling errors

1 Use your written work from a variety of subjects to find and note down your most recent personal spelling errors. Write down how you spelled the word and the correct spelling.

2 Raj has listed the spelling errors he has made in his geography book in the last three weeks. Can you spot a pattern to his mistakes? What advice could you give Raj?

✗ locasion	✗ pollusion	✗ situasion	✗ erotion	✗ contry	✗ rurral
✓ location	✓ pollution	✓ situation	✓ erosion	✓ country	✓ rural

3 Now look at your *own* list of personal errors. Are there any patterns? Once you have worked these out, go back to the relevant units to refresh your memory about spelling rules and strategies that would help you.

Activity 2 Setting personal targets

Write down *three* spelling targets for yourself. Put the date next to them and return to them at a set time in the future to see if you've been successful.

Raj's three targets looked like this:

- I will re-read the tips for spelling *-cian*, *-tion*, *-ssion* and *-sion* words and apply them to my writing so I make fewer mistakes with words with the 'shun' sound.
- I will use the apostrophe of possession correctly for all single nouns. Once I've achieved this, I'll set myself a target to use it correctly for plural nouns.
- I will remember to put the apostrophe in the right place when I miss letters out of contracted words, especially *they're*, *we're* and *you're*.

Activity 3 Going back to the beginning!

Review the main strategies for improving spelling (pages 178–180). Have you been using them in all subject areas?

Note down three spelling strategies that you find most useful. Then decide which spelling strategy you don't yet use, which might help you to spell more words correctly. Add it to your list of spelling targets. Use it to make your spelling even better!